The Biology of Insects

Studies in the Biological Sciences
General Editor: *Professor V. Moses*

Freshwater Biology: *L. G. Willoughby*
Microbial Plant Pathology: *P. J. Whitney*

The Biology of Insects

C. P. Friedlander

Pica Press   New York

Published in the United States of America in 1977 by
PICA PRESS
Distributed by Universe Books
381 Park Avenue South, New York, N.Y. 10016

Library of Congress Catalog Card Number: 76-20407
ISBN 0-87663-720-9

Printed in Great Britain

To my wife

Contents

Preface

It would be difficult to justify yet another book about insects unless it performed a function not fulfilled elsewhere. The general public is well served with books on identification and habits, while undergraduates and advanced level students have access to text book information on the morphology and physiology of the locust and cockroach. This book sets out partly to fill the very large gap that exists in the information available to students about the nature of insects as animals that are perfectly and widely adapted to life on land, and the influence on man's economy that stems from the perfection of their adaptation. The book lays no claim to being encyclopedic about economic entomology or anything else, neither is it a handbook on pest control: it tries to set out the principles which govern the success of the insects and our means of controlling the pest species. I have tried to give enough background information with which to clothe the principles, many of which are applicable to biology in general and not only to insects. The field is so vast that I have been highly selective, choosing those aspects of insect biology which either interest me most or are of very general application.

The aim has been to provide up-to-date and reliable information. It will, I believe, be evident from the text whether information is established or speculative. Since this is not a work of research I considered it unnecessary to quote an authority for every fact or opinion. Instead I have referred to works which the student will in practice find useful. They include some that are unlikely to be found outside specialist libraries and more general ones that are easily obtainable. I have given the scientific names of species as accurately as possible, but have not thought it necessary, in a work of this kind, to quote authors' names.

It was not easy to decide how high to pitch the text. I have assumed an advanced level knowledge of biology, but to-day when study of the subcellular aspects of the subject leave so little time for natural history and for knowing the organisms as organisms, it is possible to graduate and yet know very little about insects as a group and have little familiarity with their classification. Chapter 2 may help to remedy this deficiency: those who have been fortunate in their childhood will not need to read it. Again, owing to students' likely lack of familiarity with the group I have usually mentioned the Order and Family of each new insect to which I refer, and have indulged in some repetition of important points and much cross-reference – a practice which more knowledgeable students will not, I hope, find irritating. The illustrations are an important feature of the book. I have tried to illustrate almost every point, usually by means of wholly original diagrams or by drawings made from specimens — some points being checked against works of reference.

It is impossible to acknowledge all the help that I have received. Thanks are due in the first place to my teachers at Imperial College, especially Professor O. W. Richards, F.R.S., who sowed the seeds of a lasting interest. Any merit which this book possesses is due to their inspiration, and its weaknesses to their student's shortcomings. Every entomologist is conscious of the debt he owes to that mine of information, A. D. Imms' *Textbook of Entomology*.

I wish to thank Mr R. Winter, senior physics master at St Edmund's College, for help with some physical aspects of insect locomotion, and the following for supplying me with information:

Professor D.S. Bertram of the London School of Hygiene and Tropical Medicine
Mr O.N. Blatchford, Research Liaison Officer and Librarian of the Forestry Commission's Forest Research Station at Alice Holt Lodge
Dr P.B. Cornwell, Director of Research, Rentokil Ltd.
Dr M. Elliott of the Insecticides and Fungicides Department, Rothamsted Experimental Station
Mr P.H. Helm, Assistant Sales Manager of the Cambridge area of Plant Protection Ltd. (I.C.I.)
Mr M.G. Howse, Divisional Information Manager of Fisons Ltd. Research Centre for Pesticides
Dr H.E. Jahnke of Universität Hohenheim (Landwirtschaftliche Hochschule)
Miss A. Lumley of the Centre for Overseas Pest Research Scientific Information and Library services
Dr T.A.M. Nash, formerly Director of the West African Institute for Tsetse Research

I could not have managed without the unfailing help of the Library staff of the Zoological Society of London and the patience of my wife who typed the manuscript.

Part I

The Conquest of the Land

Chapter 1
The Major Features of Structure and Physiology in Relation to Terrestrial Life

Animals exist on land in a state of continuous peril. They depend for their survival on a multitude of physiological, morphological and behavioural adaptations which compensate for the loss of their ancestral aquatic environment either by simulating its features or by isolating their bodies from the dangers of the terrestrial environment.

The most obvious problem in the change from water to land is the difference between a dense buoyant medium and a rarefied one, which calls for the most profound changes in methods of support and locomotion and is possible only in the presence of a certain degree of pre-adaptation. In addition the difference between the environments imposes physiological stresses.

Aquatic environments offer equable conditions not violently disturbed by diurnal and seasonal variations. Conditions in the sea are the most constant of all, but most fresh-water environments are nearly always much less variable than even the most favourable terrestrial ones. The chief disparities are in osmotic potential, temperature, humidity and light.

The greatest hazard of all on land, and the most immediate, is that of excessive water loss leading to lethal changes in osmotic potential and salt balance. This hazard manifests itself by water loss over the general body surface and, in particular, from those regions which, in order to permit gaseous exchange and the removal of soluble metabolites, must be permeable.

We shall first consider how the insect protects itself from general water loss.

The cuticle

Insects are, for reasons which will be discussed later, small compared with many other land animals. Most are very small indeed, and consequently have a high surface area:volume ratio. In dry air they would quickly lose enough water by direct evaporation to kill them but for a feature of their cuticle which has given them almost complete freedom from this danger — the impermeability of the epicuticle.

In Figure 1.1 we see the structure of a generalized insect integument. The entire cuticle is a secretion of the epidermal cells. It consists of two distinct parts, the epicuticle and the procuticle, the principal distinction between them being that chitin is absent from the former whilst it is an essential constituent of the

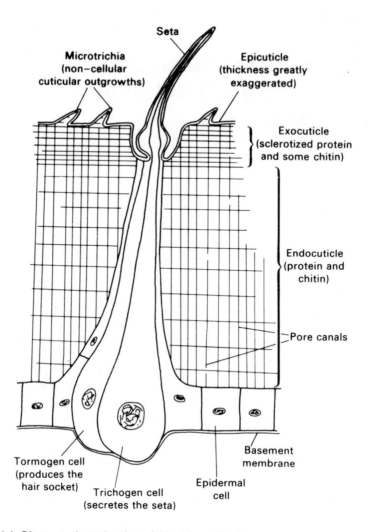

Figure 1.1 *Diagrammatic section through insect integument*

latter (Figure 1.2). Outside the epicuticle there is a monomolecular layer of lipid overlaid by an outermost layer of 'cement'. The cement and lipid layers are secreted after ecdysis and are not considered to be strictly part of the cuticle. All the same this extra-cuticular material may be very important because the main barrier to water loss is *probably* the lipid monolayer of tightly packed molecules, though other regions of the cuticle also strongly resist water loss.[1] The cement layer is impregnated with wax, which penetrates into it by means of wax canals in the epicuticle. This wax, emerging on the surface, gives rise to the 'bloom' which is characteristic of many insect cuticles. It is possible that the shiny bloom plays a part in reflecting heat from the insect's surface. Not only does the cuticle normally prevent water loss, but in some cases it allows water to enter the body. Mealworm larvae can take in water from a saturated atmosphere, and droplets of water placed

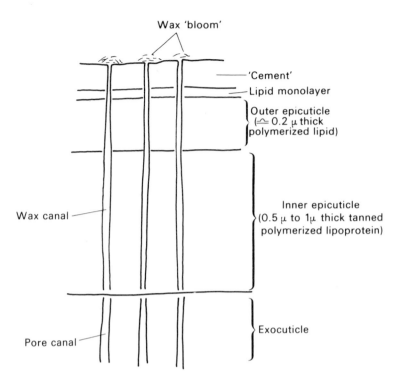

Figure 1.2 *Diagrammatic section through the epicuticle* (not drawn to scale)

on a cockroach's cuticle become covered with a layer of grease.[2] This phenomenon occurs more readily at high temperatures, which suggests that some change has occurred in the state of the wax in the canals.

The epicuticle

Epicuticle is the first part of the new integument to be formed at ecdysis. It is laid down in folds, to allow for extension as the larva increases in volume, which is the external sign of growth. It consists of a very thin outer layer and a thicker inner layer of $0.5\ \mu$ or more. Not only does the epicuticle differ from the procuticle but its outer and inner layers differ both in structure and in function.

It seems that the outer epicuticle, as the first region of the new cuticle to be formed at ecdysis, exerts a great controlling effect on the future shape of the insect. In addition it is the most chemically resistant part of the cuticle, being composed of highly polymerized lipid whose chains are arranged at right angles to the surface as in cell membranes. It is secreted in the form of many small plates from the tips of microvilli which project from the epidermal cells. These plates coalesce to form the outer epicuticle which is folded in such a way as to determine the ultimate shape of the ecdysed insect after it has expanded.

The inner epicuticle consists of tanned polymerized lipoprotein: its mode of formation is not yet fully understood.

The procuticle

General remarks about the composition of the insect procuticle must be treated
with caution for we are dealing with the largest group in the animal kingdom and
cannot expect any statement to have universal validity, in addition to which this is
a relatively new field of study and knowledge is accumulating fast. It is already
clear that the structure and composition of procuticle varies not only between
different species but also amongst members of a species, in different parts of the
individual's body and at different stages of the individual's life. It is only to be
expected that a structure of such basic importance to the insect body plan will
reflect the many different functional demands which are made on it.

The procuticle is differentiated into exo and endocuticle; in each region the poly-
saccaride α—chitin is associated with proteins, which serve as a matrix in which
chitin microfibrils are embedded.

When first secreted the entire procuticle is in the endocuticle condition; subsequently a large proportion of it is hardened to varying degrees to form the exocuticle. Some of the endocuticle always remains unhardened in the region between
the hard plates, or sclerites, of the integument in order to allow for articulation at
joints; these areas are the arthrodial membranes.

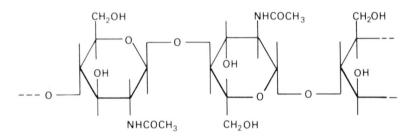

Figure 1.3 *A portion of an α—chitin molecule*

In many insects the endocuticle has a layered appearance. The chitin molecules
are long and unbranched (Figure 1.3). They are secreted by the epidermal cells in
the form of microfibrils which arrange themselves in lamellae. To be exact that
statement applies only to layers which are laid down at night: layers secreted in daytime are thinner and non-lamellate. (This fact provides a means of determining the
exact age of a larva, the daily growth layers serving a purpose similar to that of the
annual rings in trees.)

The microfibrils are arranged in helicoidal systems so that at successive levels
in a lamella they extend in different directions. It is the twist through $180°$ that
produces the lamellar appearance in the night-growth layers when viewed with
polarized light (Figure 1.4).[3] In the day-growth layers the microfibrils all lie in one
direction, known as the preferred direction. It seems likely that there is no break in
the microfibrils between regions of helicoidal systems and of preferred direction,
but that microfibrils may extend from the epidermis to the outer edge of the
procuticle, the end of one microfibril being joined to the beginning of the next. A
remarkable fact which has emerged from recent research is that the microfibrils in

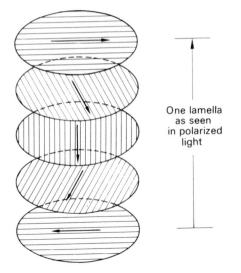

One lamella
as seen
in polarized
light

Figure 1.4 *A diagram to illustrate helicoidal structure*: the parallel lines represent microfibrils (modified after Neville and Caveney)

the helicoidal system (and often those in the preferred layer too) always twist in the same direction irrespective of whether they are on the left or right side of the animal. The cause of the insect skeleton's asymmetry at this level of structure is probably the crystallization of the chitin; its molecular structure is such that it twists in a certain fashion which in turn imparts a twist to the entire microfibril.

The main constituent of cuticle is the protein of the amorphous matrix which, like the chitin, is secreted from the epidermis. Less is known of its origin and method of secretion than in the case of the chitin; it does seem, however, that many proteins are involved and that they differ in various parts of the body. The best understood protein is the rubber-like resilin which plays an important role in imparting elasticity to the flight mechanism of the thorax. It also forms a large part of the procuticle in parts of the body which, not serving a protective function, do not need to be hardened. There is usually less protein in the endocuticle than in the exocuticle.

The endocuticle is not fully formed at the time of ecdysis, but continues to grow after each moult. This applies even to the final moult, so that it is not strictly true to say that adult insects do not grow. It has been shown that in the locust the mass of the skeleton increases three times after the final moult as a result of the continued production of endocuticle.

The endocuticle between joints, which acts as the arthrodial membrane, consists of chitin and fibrous material: it has not been studied in detail.

The net result of the procuticle's lamellar structure, consisting of twisted microfibrils with no cross-bonding, is a skeletal material which is readily bent but not easily torn: it is soft but solid, and, of course, commits the organism to stepped growth with ecdysis. This structure is sufficient for the deeper part of the integument but will not do for the outer part where, in the region of the protective sclerites, exocuticle is developed.

The exocuticle differs from the endocuticle both in its higher protein content and in the fact that the protein molecules are cross-linked to form a hard layer, whereas the endocuticle is soft and flexible. The chemistry of this hardening or *sclerotization* is too complex to be discussed here; much doubt exists about the pathways. The essential features seem to be that dihydric phenols (which are plentiful in the cuticle) diffuse outwards through the pore canals to the epicuticle, where they travel in the wax canals. There they are oxidized to quinones which diffuse back to the inner epicuticle and the exocuticle, tanning them. The tanning process involves the formation of quinonoid proteins by the terminal linking of two protein chains, followed by cross links at intermediate points along the length of the chains. The result is a substance hard enough to enable the jaws of many insects to bite through the metal foil which is used for wrapping stored foodstuffs.

Respiration

We have seen how the insect guards against general water loss by means of an overall waterproof covering. Gaseous exchange calls for respiratory surfaces whose properties are similar in all animals; they must be thin, permeable to oxygen and carbon dioxide, moist and of large surface area in relation to the volume of the tissues to be served. In addition they must either be vascularized or have some other means of readily exchanging gases with the tissues. It follows that all the features which make for good respiratory surfaces are inimical to water conservation. Insects have met the problem in an almost unique way, shared only by some other terrestrial arthropods and, in a sense, by the higher plants: the tracheal system with spiracular apertures.

Spiracles are provided with devices which can control the size of the spiracular apertures. The main function of these valves is to restrict the time that the spiracles are open to the minimum necessary for effective gaseous exchange and consequently to keep water loss to a minimum. The efficacy of this system can be demonstrated by placing insects in a desiccator, timing their survival at different temperatures, and comparing the results with those of similar tests on woodlice and myriapods. It is found that insects survive much longer than other arthropods of similar volume. If the insects are kept active their survival time is reduced, because the need for greater gaseous exchange causes the spiracles to open.

Insects, therefore, can stand the heat of the day. They can remain inactive in exposed situations, or move from place to place in search of food, even in very hot weather. In practice not all species are active throughout the twenty four hours, but that is often because of ecological adaptation — for example to avoid predators, or to match the period of nectar flow of their main food crop — rather than because their respiratory water loss situation has driven them to it. In this respect, as in so many others, insects have kept their options open.

Insects manage on rather few spiracles, typically two pairs on the thorax and eight pairs on the abdomen though the latter number is often smaller. It is hard to

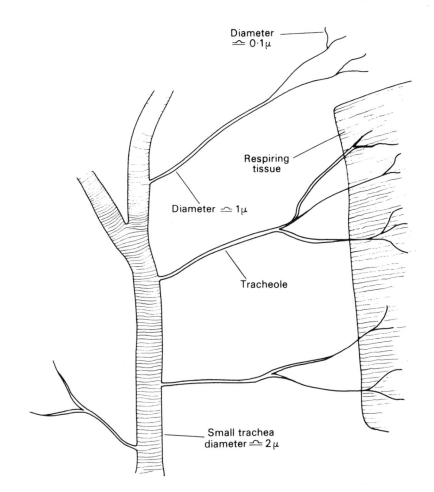

Diameter
≃ 0·1µ

Respiring
tissue

Diameter ≃ 1µ

Tracheole

Small trachea
diameter ≃ 2 µ

Figure 1.5 *Trachea supplying a respiring tissue*

imagine so few small openings permitting the entry of enough oxygen to aerate a
liquid oxygen-carrying medium, since diffusion would be too slow. Instead, by
means of the tracheae which lead in from the spiracles, and of the tracheoles into
which they divide, air is transported right into the tissues to the very site of
respiration (Figure 1.5). All true insects possess a tracheal system but the
Collembola (springtails) do not. They are able to do without one because their
small size allows them to exchange gases adequately over the general body surface,
their cuticle being permeable to oxygen and carbon dioxide as well as to water.
They have to confine themselves to moist environments.

The entire tracheal system is an invagination of the epidermis lined with cuticle
throughout, even to the finest branches of the tracheoles. The entire cuticular lining
of the *tracheae* is shed at each ecdysis. Since all internal tissues are abundantly provided with tracheolar endings it follows that all available space within the body is
exploited by the tracheal system. The spiracles of each side are linked longitudinally

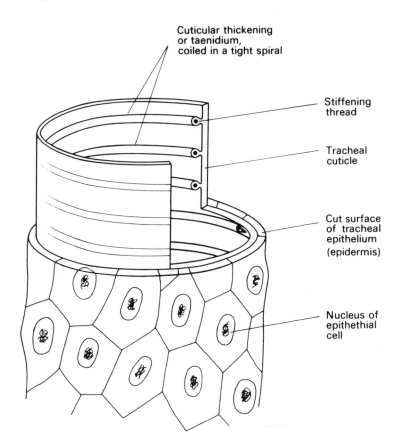

Cuticular thickening
or taenidium,
coiled in a tight spiral

Stiffening
thread

Tracheal
cuticle

Cut surface
of tracheal
epithelium
(epidermis)

Nucleus of
epithethial
cell

Figure 1.6 *A diagram to show relationship of cuticular lining and tracheal epithelium*

by large tubes, the tracheal trunks, and in many insects many thin-walled dilatable airsacs arise both from the trunks and from the tracheae themselves. Clearly, muscular movements may either squeeze or stretch the tracheal system, tending to cut off the supply of air in a random manner. In order to resist the worst effects of compression the walls of the tracheae are strengthened in the manner of an armoured hose, by spiral threads which are laid down in cuticular thickenings of the tracheal and tracheolar lining (Figure 1.6). Consequently a pull on the trachea may cause it to stretch, but not to break, and although the diameter will be temporarily reduced the lumen is not obliterated. The situation resembles that of the protoxylem in seed plants, whose spiral thickening allows the vessels to elongate below the stem or root apex. This thickening is absent from the airsacs which serve to compensate for the effects of compression on other parts of the system.

The tracheae are based on a cylinder of epidermal cells, but the tracheoles to which they give rise have a different nature. Tracheoles are single cells, and their lumen is intracellular. The single cells may be as much as 300—400 μ long, and, penetrating deep into cells and muscle fibres come in close proximity to their mitochondria. The tracheoles end blindly, the terminal section being filled with liquid and the remainder with air. In the tissues a simple but effective governing mechanism comes into operation: the extent to which air is drawn into the tissues is controlled by the extent of their need for it. The metabolites which are produced as a result of muscular contraction are hypertonic to the haemolymph or general body fluid, so that a period of exertion is followed by a withdrawal of water from all cells that are bathed in haemolymph, which includes the tracheolar cells. Consequently water is withdrawn from the tracheolar vacuole and the column of air takes its place, bringing oxygen closer to the mitochondria of the muscles and enabling the oxygen debt to be cleared (Figure 1.7). This mechanism presumably has the added advantage of making it possible for air to be brought to tissues which particularly need it in preference to those which have not accumulated an oxygen debt; it is not an indiscriminate increase of air to all tissues, and must be a desirable feature when the supply of air is temporarily limited.

Insects consume a large supply of oxygen in a short time when they fly. Active

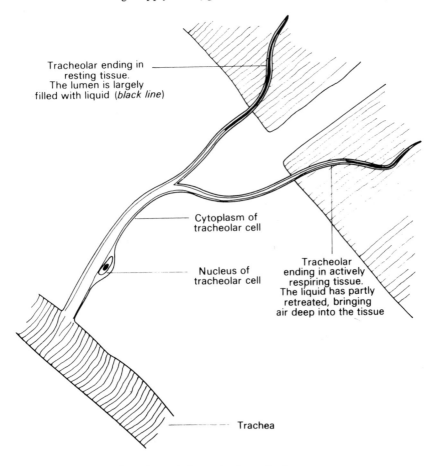

Tracheolar ending in resting tissue. The lumen is largely filled with liquid (*black line*)

Cytoplasm of tracheolar cell

Nucleus of tracheolar cell

Tracheolar ending in actively respiring tissue. The liquid has partly retreated, bringing air deep into the tissue

Trachea

Figure 1.7 *A diagram to show air supply by tracheoles to the tissues*

insects usually assist the intake of air by means of forcing it through the tracheal system rather than by letting it enter by passive diffusion, which is sufficient for small, sluggish insects. Large active ones, however, cause air to travel through the system, often in a directed manner by drawing it in through some of the spiracles and forcing it out through others.

We can now see how the tracheal system fulfils the requirements of a good respiratory surface (page 18).

Features of a good respiratory surface.	The insects' solution by means of the tracheal system.
Thinness	The average diameter of a tracheole is approximately $0·5\ \mu$. The thickness of its cuticular lining is therefore very small indeed.
Permeability to oxygen and carbon dioxide	Unsclerotized cuticle is permeable to oxygen and even more so to carbon dioxide.
Moisture	The tracheoles are buried in the tissues and are permanently moist.
Large surface area	The total area of the tracheoles (which *are* the respiratory surfaces) is great because the tracheoles are numerous.
Means of exchanging gases with the tissues	Since the tracheoles penetrate into tissue cells no liquid circulatory system is needed for transport of oxygen and carbon dioxide.

Insects which have secondarily reverted to aquatic life as adults retain the tracheal system and breathe in essentially the same manner as do terrestrial insects, coming to the surface for air. Indeed many insects which live in water as adults can also walk on land, and fly (Chapter 4).

Aquatic larvae, too, possess the tracheal system although they do not leave the water except, in some cases, when they are about to pupate. All degrees of adaptation to aquatic life exist (Figure 1.8): some larvae rise to the surface and expose their functional spiracles to the air, others possess thin outgrowths of the body (gills) which are in close contact with tracheae although the spiracles are non-functional, whilst yet others have no gills but merely carry out gaseous exchange across the general body surface under which ramifies a network of fine tracheae.

Excretion

All animals dispel water in the process of removing from their bodies the waste products of metabolism. In the case of nitrogenous excretion, with which we shall be principally concerned in this account, water may be lost in large quantities. That

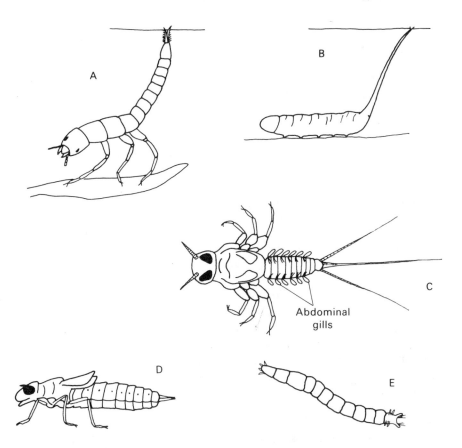

Figure 1.8 *Respiration in some aquatic larvae* **A** Larva of a dytiscid beetle **B** Maggot of a hover-fly (Syrphidae): most syrphid larvae are aquatic. In both dytiscid and syrphid larvae air is drawn into the tracheal system through the terminal spiracles which break the water surface by means of unwettable hairs. **C** Ephemeropteran larva (nymph): abdominal gills, covered in thin cuticle, are kept in constant motion. The spiracles are sealed. **D** Nymph of anisopteran dragonfly: water is drawn through the anus into the rectum which is lined with leaf-like gills containing tracheae. The spiracles are sealed. **E** Bloodworm larva of a chironomid fly: the spiracles are sealed and oxygen diffuses across the cuticle straight into the tracheae. In addition the blood contains haemoglobin, which is exceptional in insects.

is unimportant for aquatic animals which can easily replace the lost water, or which may even find it useful to combine the process of excretion with that of removing excess water by producing a very dilute urine, but it presents a serious problem for terrestrial ones. Organs of nitrogenous excretion usually play a part both in osmoregulation and in regulating the salt balance, and insects are no exception. The principal organs are Malpighian tubules, blindly-ending simple tubular ducts which open into the alimentary canal where the mesenteron joins the hindgut, (Figure 1.9) but the product of the tubules is further modified as it travels towards the anus. As one might expect in so large a group as the insects there is great variety in the arrangement of the tubules and in the nature of their secretion, but in a general way the principle is that the tubules serve to extract water, urate, sodium and potassium

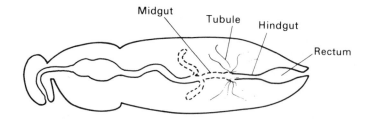

Figure 1.9 *The position of the Malpighian tubules in most insects:* they lie freely in the haemocoel (The mesenteron is shown by dotted lines.)

from the haemocoel, subsequently converting the urate into uric acid which needs no water for its removal from the body. Most of the water and the useful ions are then returned to the haemolymph, while the uric acid is expelled through the alimentary canal.

Since insects live in many different habitats and since the habits of the developing stages may differ wholly from those of the adults we find many variations on the general process described above. The excretory system gives an admirable example of physiological adaptation within a group. The problems of aquatic larvae and of aphids, which ingest large quantities of water, are different from those of most terrestrial insects and are answered in completely different ways.

Much of our detailed knowledge comes from the study of only a few insects especially dipteran larvae, the locust and the blood-sucking bug, *Rhodnius*. The account of excretion which follows is a synthesis of information from various sources and is probably a fair picture of what happens in many insects.

The tubules lie freely in the haemocoel and, being overlaid with some muscle cells, are able to wriggle slightly which probably helps to bring them into intimate contact with the haemolymph. Tracheae run along their length, which suggests that an active process is occurring in them. A tubule is lined with a single layer of cells, containing many mitochondria, and their inner surface is composed of microvilli, (Figure 1.10), into which extend many more mitochondria. The presence of plentiful mitochondria strengthens the inference that an active secretory or absorptive process is associated with these cells. The tubules lead into the hindgut

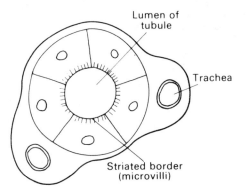

Figure 1.10 *A transverse section of a Malpighian tubule*

595.7   F913b   c.1

or 'intestine' which, unlike them is lined by a thin layer of cuticle. It is thrown into folds lengthwise, as is the rectum, and therefore has a large surface area. The rectum, in particular, is abundantly provided with tracheae, and with musculature.

The acidity of the tubules and rectum can be estimated by inserting dyes. Whereas the tubules' reaction is alkaline or, towards the end of the proximal portion, slightly acidic, that of the rectum is highly acidic.

The tubular fluid is isosmotic with the haemolymph, but of different composition. Whereas the potassium concentration in the tubules is much higher than in the haemolymph the reverse is true of sodium, chloride and most other ions. It seems that potassium may be a key factor in the flow of water from the haemolymph to the tubules, for an increase in the potassium level of the haemolymph (which can be induced by adding potassium chloride to the insects' drinking water) is accompanied by a rise in the rate of flow of tubular fluid. The potassium is actively secreted into the tubules and is thought then to cause the entry of water by a mechanism which is not fully understood but may be electro-osmotic (passage of water owing to potential difference across the tubule wall) or due to frictional interaction with the incoming potassium ions. Whatever the method, the effect is to produce a strong flow of fluid along the tubules towards the gut with the resultant physical removal of the tubules' contents. These contents consist of the various organic components of the haemolymph: sugars, amino acids and the excretory substances which are principally urates.

An analogy may be drawn between the action of the tubules and of the glomerulus of a mammal. In each case there is an outflow of body fluid accompanied by the potential loss not only of many useful organic and inorganic substances but also of the water which is vital to a terrestrial animal. What the mammal achieves by virtue of ultra-filtration, in consequence of a high blood pressure, the insect achieves by active secretion. There is one important difference though, that the tubules can be more selective: salt balance is achieved there because inorganic salts which are present in excess can escape into the tubule by a process of passive diffusion.

Just as the mammalian kidney has to provide a means of restoring to the blood most of the water and the 'useful' substances which would otherwise be lost, the insect must solve the same problem. The analogue of the tubules' loop of Henlé and the collecting duct is the insect's rectum, and to a lesser extent its intestine. If the main function of the Malpighian tubules is secretion, that of the rectum is osmoregulation through reabsorption.

The osmotic pressure of the rectal fluid is higher than that of the haemolymph owing to extraction of water from the rectal wall against an osmotic gradient. In the locust it has been shown that electro-osmosis cannot be responsible. It seems that withdrawal of water from the rectum is another active transport process.

The result of loss of water from the rectum is that the concentration of urate increases greatly. Owing to the strongly acidic reaction of the rectum uric acid is precipitated and accumulates, eventually forming a large lump which is egested with the faeces. In this manner the insect succeeds in removing its nitrogenous waste with great economy of water. These events are summed up in Figure 1.11.

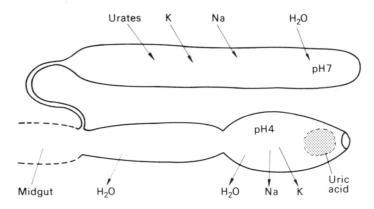

Figure 1.11 *Changes in acidity and composition along the length of a Malpighian tubule, intestine and rectum*

Another adaptation for water conservation is the cryptonephridial arrangement of the tubules which occurs in many insects (Figure 1.12). The distal portion lies close against the rectal wall to which it is bound by a sheath. Among the beetles it is found that this arrangement is characteristic of those which have the greatest need to conserve water: those whose need is less have the tubules lying free in the haemocoel. The suggestion is that water can readily be extracted from the rectum and used for flushing the tubules – a further step in economy.

We have compared the insects' excretory problem with that of mammals. There is also some similarity in the way water loss is controlled, but in this respect much less is known about the action of hormones in insects than in mammals.

The best known example of an insect diuretic hormone is in *Rhodnius*. *Rhodnius* is a blood-sucking bug (Hemiptera: Heteroptera) which takes large meals at intervals of several days. Immediately after the meal it is in a similar situation to the aphid, needing to remove a large quantity of water which has been absorbed into the haemolymph from the gut. For this purpose urine flows rapidly, but afterwards it virtually stops, although the Malpighian tubules continue to pour their contents into the rectum. It has been shown that a diuretic hormone produced in neurosecretory cells of the thoracic ganglia permits the rapid flow, after which the rate falls to the low level that is normal in terrestrial insects and is associated with the formation of granules of uric acid in the rectum. The diuretic hormone evidently increases the permeability of the rectum or perhaps, in the case of

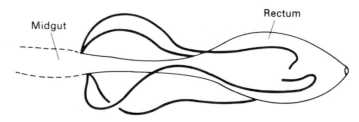

Figure 1.12 *The cryptonephridial condition:* the distal ends of the Malpighian tubules (in heavy black) are in close contact with the rectum.

Rhodnius, of the proximal region of the tubules from which water is certainly with-drawn. It is likely that water balance is influenced by hormones in other insects as well.

We have seen that uricotely (the excretion of nitrogen in the form of uric acid) is a valuable means of conserving water in a terrestrial animal. Uric acid is the end product of nitrogen metabolism in the vast majority of insects, including those which live partly or wholly in water. Ammonotely (excretion of ammonia) occurs amongst several aquatic larvae, eg those of *Sialis* (the alder fly), Odonata (dragon-flies) and Trichoptera (caddisflies), but in each case it is a secondary adaptation to aquatic life, and the adults are uricotelic. In these aquatic forms ammonia is found to occur in the rectal fluid, but not in the tubules. The aquatic larvae are particularly well suited to ammonotely because they can use their large respiratory surfaces as excretory ones too (Figure 1.8).

Not all aquatic larvae are ammonotelic: mosquito larvae excrete uric acid, which may be correlated with the fact that in the Diptera as a whole aquatic larvae are the exception rather than the rule.

Aphids are among the very few insects which do not possess Malpighian tubules. They are exceptional among terrestrial animals in being ammonotelic. They are able to dispose of their nitrogenous waste by diluting it to a safe level, in the large volume of water which they ingest from their plant hosts, and exuding it in the honey-dew. This is a special adaptation: from the point of view of their excretion aphids are virtually aquatic!

Flight

The power of flight is the most characteristic feature of insects and has made them the dominant invertebrates. It is the feature that has made them even more success-ful than the Chelicerata ($\equiv$ Arachnida) which almost match them in the complexity of their instinctive behaviour and in their general adaptation to terrestrial life. Whereas morphological and physiological adaptations (such as the Chelicerata's effective locomotion and their ability to resist desiccation) enable organisms to accommodate themselves to many different environments, the ability to fly enables insects in addition to exchange one habitat for another: it increases their power of dispersal, of escape from predators and of access to food supplies. Migration on a large scale becomes possible, and with it the opportunity of exploiting food sources to their utmost. It also offers better chances for mixture in the gene pool.

Flight is characteristic of all but the most primitive Orders of insects, in which the apterous condition is primitive, that is to say those whose ancestors never possessed wings. Such insects live mainly in the soil and, apart from the Collembola which some consider not to be insects at all, have a relatively unimportant part to play in the economy of nature. Amongst the Orders of winged insects (Pterygota), however, aptery may occur as the result of adaptation to special circumstances. Nearly all the Orders include some members that are secondarily apterous (eg many aphids among the Hemiptera, ants among the Hymenoptera) and some Orders are wholly apterous and highly adapted to parasitic existence (eg fleas and lice).

Apterous Pterygota, are, of course, restricted by their adaptation but, unlike the Apterygota, exert a great influence on the environment to which they are adapted. In nearly all cases it is possible to relate their morphological features to those of winged forms from which they are believed to have diverged in the comparatively recent past. In one of the most important wingless Orders, the fleas, it has been shown that the special jumping modification makes use of features of the former wing mechanism.

Wings evolved in the Carboniferous (Chapter 3). It is believed that the process occurred once only, so that all subsequent winged insects are descended from the group in which the phenomenon evolved. The reason for this belief is that throughout the winged insects the flight mechanism employs homologous parts of the skeleton and the neuromuscular system, although they are not used in the same way in the various Orders.

The more primitive insects employ a simpler flight mechanism than do the higher forms, but not necessarily a less effective one; the large dragonflies, although primitive, are amongst the fastest of fliers.

Flight is difficult to discuss briefly since it involves almost every organ system. We shall not consider here its aerodynamics or the actual movement of the wings, a lucid account of which the reader will find in Nachtigall,[4] but shall look at a few physiological implications of a mode of locomotion that has so rarely been evolved.

All insect muscle is of the striated type, much of it resembling vertebrate striated muscle. In the more primitive insects the flight muscles retain their similarity to those of the normal muscles of the thorax, abdomen and legs. Generally speaking these are the insects which rely heavily on direct flight muscles for moving the wings, that is to say on the muscles which have their origin in the ventral exoskeleton and are directly inserted into the base of the wings. There is one set of muscles for forcing the wing down and another for producing the up-beat, a typical antagonistic arrangement in which the wings are moved as though they were limbs. This manner of causing the wings to beat is adequate in insects which fly weakly or slowly. The fibres of such muscles are said to be of the tubular type, from their appearance in transverse section (Figure 1.13) when a group of myofibrils is seen radiating from a clear central region of sarcoplasm. The width of such a fibre is about 20 μ.

The flight muscles of dragonflies are tubular too, but they are modified, having wider myofibrils and much larger mitochondria which are packed all round the myofibrils and permit the release of more energy. A dragonfly's direct flight musculature moves the wings at about twenty beats per second, enough to propel the insect at twenty five kilometres per hour. It is not strictly correct to attribute this achievement to the musculature: the elastic protein, resilin, plays an important part. Resilin forms the substance of the cuticle at the wing hinge, and its natural elasticity, returning most of the energy which has been loaded into it by muscular contraction, greatly reduces the total amount of work required from the muscles.

The locust has a more advanced system. Its wings are moved by a combination of direct and indirect flight muscles, the latter being wholly responsible for the up-stroke. Indirect muscles transmit their pull not to the wings but to the walls of the thoracic box, distorting it first in one way and then in another. The action results in

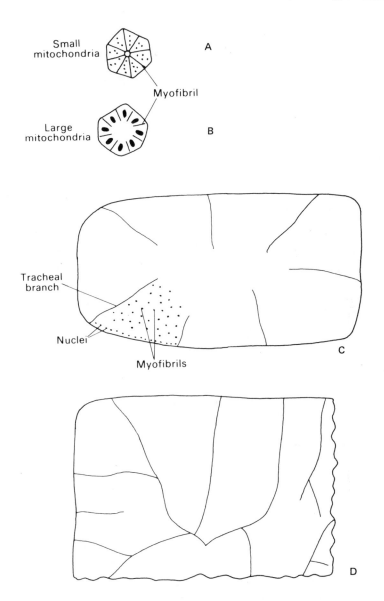

Figure 1.13 *Types of insect muscle fibre* (diagrammatic but not to scale) **A** Tubular type: as in leg muscle fibre and cockroach flight muscle fibre. **B** Tubular type: as in dragonfly flight muscle fibre. **C** Close-packed type: as in grasshopper flight muscle fibre. **D** Fibrillar type: as in house-fly flight muscle fibre (only a quarter of the cross sectional area is shown).

the wings being moved passively owing to their being hinged between two regions of the thoracic box, the tergum and pleura, which are displaced in relation to each other (Figure 1.14). The continuous change and restoration of the shape of the thorax is not the result merely of muscular pull causing flexure of arthrodial

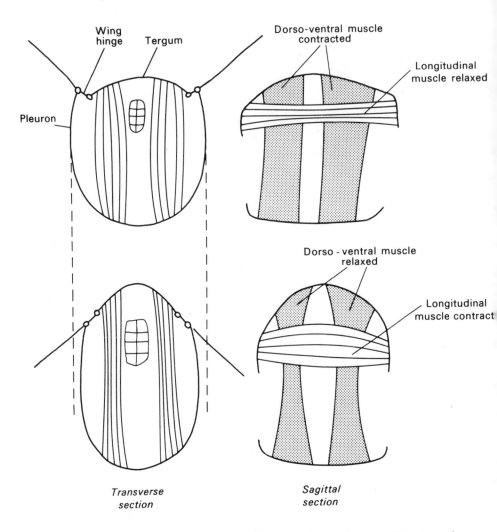

Figure 1.14 *Action of indirect flight muscles* (diagrammatic, the distortion of the thorax is greatly exaggerated).

membranes. Resilin is present in other parts of the thoracic wall besides the wing hinge so that the entire thoracic box acts as a storehouse of the energy supplied by the muscles.

The wing beats operate on a click mechanism (Figure 1.15). Where the wing joins the thorax there is a series of pivots. The wing-base is attached to the wing-bearing sclerite (shown stippled) which articulates with the edge of the pleuron at the pleural wing process. The wing-bearing sclerite articulates with the parascutal shelf which in turn articulates with the massive part of the tergum. At position **B** the two sclerites are in line and the wing is in its mid-way position. The sclerites can be held in this linear position indefinitely provided that some pressure be applied to at least one end of the system. It is the function of the pleurosternal muscle to

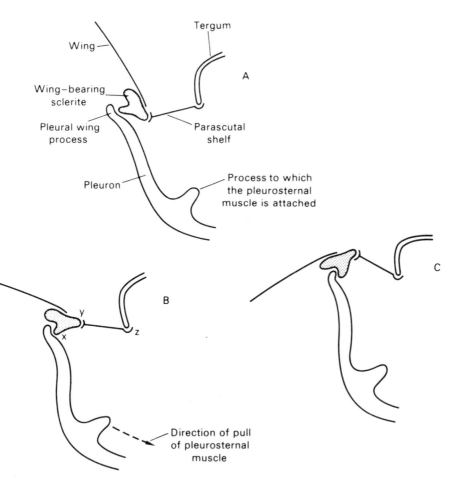

Figure 1.15 *The click mechanism* (slightly adapted from Nachtigall)

supply the necessary pull: this muscle is relaxed when the insect is grounded and contracts before flight begins, pulling the pleuron inwards and 'setting' the click mechanism. We can imagine as an analogy a mountaineer jammed horizontally, face downwards, in a crevice between two vertical rock faces. By keeping his arms and legs fully extended he can just bridge the gap: if his knees give way his precarious equilibrium is lost and he falls. Similarly any distortion of the thoracic wall which leads to a downward pressure at **y** will tip the system into position **A**. Further muscular distortion of the thorax operates a lever system which then lifts the sclerites once more into a linear position, and stresses the system by applying pressure against the pleural wing process. The resilin at the hinge stores the energy, and the system remains stable until further distortion of the thorax applies an upward pressure at **y** and the wing flicks down. When the lever mechanism forces the sclerites into a linear position again the process is repeated until the wing flicks up. The resilin has functioned in two ways: at the hinge it has acted as a spring to deliver a sudden *click* and, in other parts of the thorax, it has served to give elasticity which magnifies the distorting action of the musculature. This account gives but the barest facts of an extremely complex system.

In the locust the effect of resilin elasticity is that about eighty six per cent of the energy which is needed on each stroke is stored for use in the next, the balance of fourteen per cent only having to be supplied by the muscles. Of this energy about twenty five per cent is stored in the wing hinge itself which, although very small, is composed almost entirely of resilin: the remainder is stored elsewhere in the thorax.

The locust's flight muscle, both direct and indirect is of a more advanced type than the dragonfly's, with larger fibres (Figure 1.13). Effective though this muscle is in combination with the elastic nature of the thorax it does not produce more rapid wing-beats than does the dragonfly's — about twenty per second. Lepidoptera too have close-packed muscle but, since locusts and butterflies are capable of long periods of uninterrupted migratory flight, the muscle is clearly able to perform steadily. Aerodynamic *drag*, the backward-acting component which opposes the forward-acting *thrust*, increases as the size of the wing and the speed of its forward movement through the air decrease. Consequently, smaller insects whose wings are not only relatively but absolutely smaller beat them faster than do larger ones, and have the most specialized energy-producing systems of all.

It is of course misleading to speak of larger and smaller insects in this context; the Diptera and Hymenoptera, in which the wing-beat is faster, contain several large species which function on the lines of the remainder of their Orders, but in a general sense it is true to say that the physical demands of small size call for a fast wing-beat.

The motive power in these insects is provided by indirect muscles. Direct flight muscles still exist but are concerned with controlling the wing-beat, not with producing it. The indirect muscle is of the type known as *fibrillar*: it differs from the close-packed type both histologically and physiologically. The fibres are so large that an entire muscle may consist, in some highly evolved flies, of as few as six. Their size demands an abundant tracheolar supply and energy source, and the mitochondria, which lie between the myofibrils, are very large.

The chief distinction between this and the other forms of flight muscle is in their rhythm. In the more primitive forms each successive muscle contraction and relaxation is stimulated by nerve impulses from the central nervous system (neurogenic rhythm), but fibrillar muscle has a myogenic rhythm. A neurogenic rhythm would be too slow to produce the beat. In myogenic rhythm the contraction is triggered off by the state of tension of the muscle itself. Contraction of the dorso-ventral muscles distorts the thorax in such a way that the longitudinal muscles are stretched. At a certain point in the distortion the click mechanism operates, producing a jerk in the thorax. The stretched longitudinal muscle responds to the jerk by contracting, and so, as long as the necessary physiological environment exists, the process continues. No nervous stimulation is involved, but the abundant innervation of the fibres serves to control the flow of calcium ions without which the energy needed for contraction would not be released.

The energy needed for flight is far greater than that which we usually associate with poikilotherms. Insects have the added problem of a small body-fluid volume, so that dissolved sugars cannot be stored in large quantities. We find therefore a correlation between an insect's behaviour and the type of energy substrate and store which it employs. The widespread animal storage carbohydrate, glycogen, is far from being universal amongst insects, though it does occur in *Drosophila*.

The great advantage of glucose or some other sugar as a substrate is its availability for use at short notice. It occurs as a storage material in many small active insects such as flies whose bursts of activity are limited to short periods. Large migratory insects such as locusts and butterflies use fat both as a storage material and, on account of its high energy content, as a respiratory substrate. Locusts are known to rely on glucose at the beginning of flight but, once started, they tap the fat body which occupies a large part of the abdomen. Bees and bumblebees, in spite of their immense activity, rely for energy entirely on sugar, which they can afford to do because they replenish themselves several times in the course of a lengthy foraging expedition.

In order that the flight muscles may produce enough power to sustain flight they have to be at an appropriate temperature, which varies with the species. Many insects simply do not fly if the ambient temperature is below the critical value; that is broadly speaking true of diurnal insects. Locusts have to orientate themselves and they tilt their bodies so as to receive maximum solar heat before they can take off. On a mild sunny summer day many hover-flies will usually be found flying near flowers, but shortly after the sun has been concealed by a cloud the flies vanish, having settled inconspicuously on the flowers: on a really hot day a short overcast period may not produce such a dramatic effect. Similarly house-flies become active indoors in winter when the central heating is switched on, and quiescent again when the temperature drops. Those insects are wholly at the mercy of the ambient temperature. The flies produce considerable heat in their flight muscles but, owing to their glossy cuticles, radiate it rapidly so that even a brief period of flightlessness on a dull day may render them unable to take off again. At times when flies are sluggish bumblebees may, however, be active. They can fly even at $0°$C. because they have evolved the ability of warming their thorax, by means of muscular contraction, up to a temperature which is adequate for flight.[5]

The problem of flight at low temperatures is shared by nocturnal insects, especially the large ones. It has been examined in the hawk moths (sphinx moths in the USA) many of which are nocturnal and large enough to be conveniently studied.[6] In their case the respiratory substrate is fat, and its metabolism in the thoracic muscles releases the necessary heat. The warming-up process resembles shivering in homiothermic animals, when rapid muscular contraction in the absence of much external work releases most of the fuel's energy as heat. The longitudinal and dorso-ventral muscles are made to contract almost simultaneously instead of alternately; the result is fast vibration of the wings through only a small arc. The bumblebee, incidentally, is even more efficient. It has a device for dissociating wing movement from the thoracic box during warming-up, so that hardly any external work is done and all energy is dissipated as heat.

Only the thorax is heated in this way; the abdomen remains at the ambient temperature. This is achieved by means of the thick covering of thoracic scales which serve the same function as hair or feathers. When the moth is actively flying its problem is to lose heat from the thorax, especially while it is hovering as it sucks nectar. Heat loss is probably achieved through circulation of body fluid by the heart which, being long and lying just below the dorsal surface of the abdomen where the covering of scales is sparse, acts as an effective heat dissipator. The rise in thoracic temperature causes the heart, through nervous stimulation, to beat faster and so to pump the overheated thoracic body-fluid away from the thorax at an increased rate to the abdomen for cooling. The heart is stimulated in this way only when the thoracic temperature tends to exceed $40°C$., just protecting the moth from the lethal temperature of about $46°C$.

Diurnal insects, of course, are liable to become overheated at times of intense activity. Locusts, in the course of long flights in hot countries, probably have an overheating problem. The solution may lie in the hairless, shiny and smooth nature of their thoracic cuticle which acts as a good conductor and radiator. Whether their heart assists in cooling, as does that of the hawk moth, is not known.

In the light of what we have said the bumblebee's thick pile of hair might be considered a source of overheating for a very active insect. It is not, partly because bumblebees are really quite small insects without their covering of hair, so that the tendency to lose heat is great, and because instead of remaining in continuous flight for very long they frequently stop to take on further supplies of nectar. Far from overheating being a danger, bumblebees expend energy to keep their flight muscles in a state of readiness for take-off even while feeding.

References

A On the cuticle

1 LOCKE,M. (1965). Permeability of insect cuticle to water and lipids. *Science* **147**, 295–298.
2 BEAMENT,J.W.L. (1964). The active and passive movement of water in insects. In *Advances in insect physiology*, Ed. J.W.L.Beament, J.E.Treherne and V.B.Wigglesworth. vol.2, 67–129. New York: Academic Press.
3 NEVILLE,A.C. & CAVENEY,S. (1969). Scarabeid beetle exocuticle as an optical analogue of cholesteric liquid crystals. *Biol.Rev.***44**, 531–562.
    For general information on the cuticle:
    NEVILLE,A.C. Cuticle ultrastructure in relation to the whole insect—and—
    WEIS-FOGH,T. Structure and formation of insect cuticle. In *Insect Ultrastructure*, Ed. A.C.Neville (1970). London: Royal Entomological Society.

B On respiration

    A standard work is:
    WIGGLESWORTH,V.B. (1965). *The principles of insect physiology*. 6th edition. ch IX. London: Methuen.
    A useful short account:
    WIGGLESWORTH,V.B. (1972). *Insect respiration*, Oxford Biology Readers 48. Oxford University Press.

C On excretion

For a full account:

STOBBART,R.H. & SHAW,J. Salt and water balance: excretion. In *The physiology of Insecta,* Ed. M.Rockstein. (1964). vol.3. New York: Academic Press.

D On flight

4 NACHTIGALL,W. (1968). *Insects in flight.* English translation 1974. London: George Allen & Unwin.

This admirable book is the only account which makes the mechanism of flight intelligible to those who are unversed in physics and mathematics.

5 HEINRICH,B. The energetics of the bumblebee. *Scientific American* April 1973.

6 HEINRICH,B. & BARTHOLOMEW,G.A. Temperature control in flying moths. *Scientific American* June 1972.

For an advanced account:

PRINGLE,J.W.S. (1957). *Insect flight.* Cambridge University Press.

PRINGLE,J.W.S. Locomotion: flight. In *The physiology of Insecta,* Ed. M.Rockstein (1965). vol.2. New York: Academic Press.

Since this book was written a lucid and simple account of flight has appeared:

PRINGLE,J.W.S. (1975). *Insect flight,* Oxford Biology Readers 52. Oxford University Press.

Chapter 2
The Variety of Insects

The purpose of this chapter is to present a general view of the vast Class of insects for those who are not familiar with its classification. It will serve as a vocabulary and means of reference for use with later chapters. We shall not attempt to describe all the groups of insects, but rather to express the salient features of the most important ones in a simple way by means of illustrations. That is feasible because the Class is subdivided largely on grounds of external morphology.

The fundamental division is into two Sub-Classes (Figure 2.1) on the basis of wing features. The Apterygota are primitively wingless, that is to say their ancestors never possessed wings. They exhibit other primitive features too: the fact that ecdysis continues throughout their lives and that they possess some abdominal appendages. In higher insects abdominal appendages are confined to the posterior segments and are greatly modified, usually in connexion with reproduction: for copulation and egg-laying.

The Sub-Class Pterygota includes all other living insects. They all had winged ancestors, though some of the living ones have lost their wings as an adaptation to some particular mode of life such as parasitism (eg fleas and lice) or because they combine with winged members of their species to form a social unit (eg wingless worker ants).

The Pterygota are composed of two Divisions based on the manner in which they develop from egg to adult. The Exopterygota are the more primitive. Their eggs hatch into larvae which usually look like miniature but wingless versions of the adults. The wings grow from wing-buds which are clearly visible externally. At the final ecdysis the wings assume their full size. This kind of development is often known as simple or incomplete metamorphosis: a better term is direct development. As a rule the larvae (often referred to as nymphs) lead similar lives to those of the adults, the main exceptions being the aquatic larvae which develop into adults that live out of water.

The Endopterygota are the most highly evolved insects. Their eggs hatch into larvae which usually, and especially in the more advanced endopterygotes, bear little or no resemblance to the adults either in structure or in their way of life. The larva when fully grown enters the externally inactive pupal stage in which the larval tissues are reorganized into those of the adult. The wings develop under the larval cuticle and are not visible until late in the pupal stage. This kind of development is often known as complex or complete metamorphosis, but indirect development is a more helpful term.

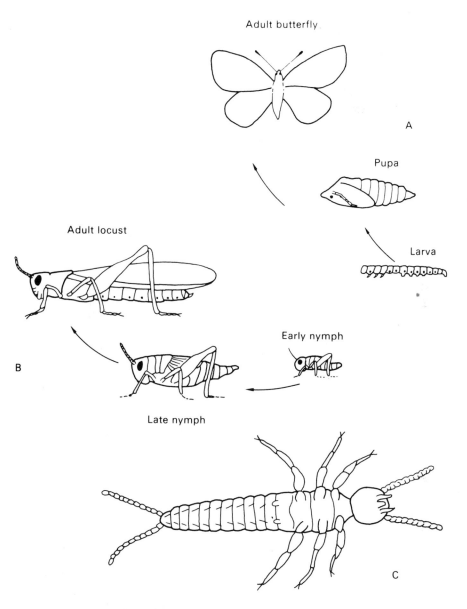

Figure 2.1 *Major divisions of the Class Insecta* **A** Endopterygota **B** Exopterygota
C Apterygota: *Campodea,* a dipluran (ventral view to show abdominal appendages)

The four Orders of Apterygota consist of very small insects, well under one centimetre in length (Figure 2.2).

The THYSANURA (Figure 2.2A) are small, have compound eyes and normal biting
mouthparts. They have small abdominal projections. The median long projection
from the last abdominal segment is perhaps homologous with the crustacean telson.

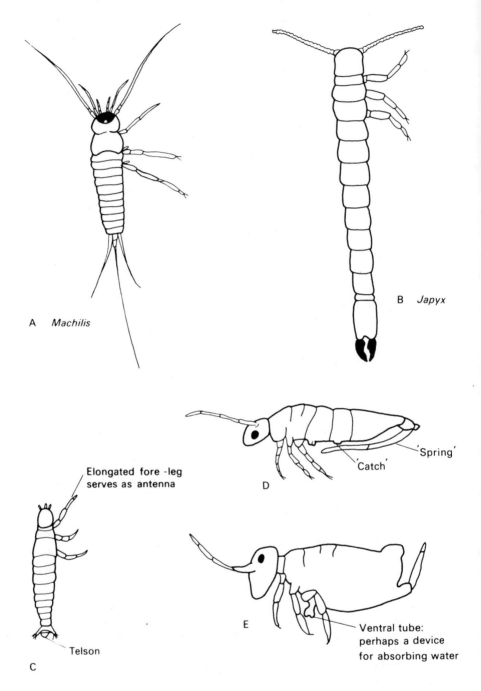

A *Machilis*

B *Japyx*

Elongated fore-leg
serves as antenna

D

'Catch'   'Spring'

Telson

C

E

Ventral tube:
perhaps a device
for absorbing water

Figure 2.2 *The Apterygota* **A** Thysanura **B** Diplura **C** Protura **D** Collembola (springtails): Sub-order Arthropleona **E** Collembola (springtails): Sub-order Symphypleona

Machilidae live under rocks on the coast and Lepismatidae occur mostly in warm parts of houses.

The DIPLURA (Figure 2.2B) are small, eyeless and have biting mouthparts which are retracted into pockets when not in use. Their antennae have segmental muscles, a very unusual feature amongst insects. Abdominal appendages are present (Figure 2.1).
Two Families are Campodeidae and Japygidae.

The PROTURA (Figure 2.2C) are very small, devoid of eyes and antennae. Their jaws are bristle-like, sunken and used for feeding on leaf juices. They are unique amongst insects in producing extra abdominal segments after hatching.

The COLLEMBOLA or springtails (Figures 2.2D and 2E) are the only Apterygota of economic importance, being probably the most abundant of all insects and playing an important role as scavengers in the soil. They lie at the base of many carnivorous food-chains.
Their jaws are sunken, their antennae have segmental muscles. Few have spiracles. They have a unique method of jumping by means of modified abdominal appendages: a 'spring' on the fourth segment is held compressed by a 'catch' on the third and, when released, hits the ground and gives the animal a large undirected leap.
The two Sub-Orders have characteristic shapes brought out by Figure 2.2.
Sminthurus viridis is a widespread and often serious pest of clover and grasses.

The Orders of Pterygota are established *in the first place* mainly on wing features. In the case of many Orders there is in addition great uniformity of mouthparts and general body structure so that subdividing them is not easy. For example in the Lepidoptera the existence of scales on the wings is the prime character: the feeding mechanism is uniform almost throughout, and the larvae are very similar. Families are determined by a study of wing venation, which calls for removal of the scales. The difficulty in the Lepidoptera arises from the uniformity of their mode of life. The Hymenoptera on the other hand are much more varied, so that there is no difficulty about dividing the Order into Sub-Orders and Families, for the same general wing form includes a considerable range of variation in body form, mouthparts and larvae. Different criteria are brought into play for establishing Families in the various Orders. For example in the Coleoptera the number of tarsal joints is often important as, in one section of the Diptera, is the position of bristles on the body.
Very rarely can a taxonomic group be established on the basis of a single feature, not even at the level of species, which is only to be expected since organisms are the result of an evolutionary process which has impinged on all aspects of their life. When, therefore we make a statement such as 'the Lepidoptera are an Order whose adults are adapted to sucking exposed juices from plants' we are saying what is broadly true but it does not apply to the most primitive ones which bite pollen grains or to the highly specialized clothes moth whose adult has virtually no mouthparts. We need to make general statements for convenience because to hedge in every remark with exceptions would make our account turgid, but we must constantly remember the limitations inherent in any biological statement.

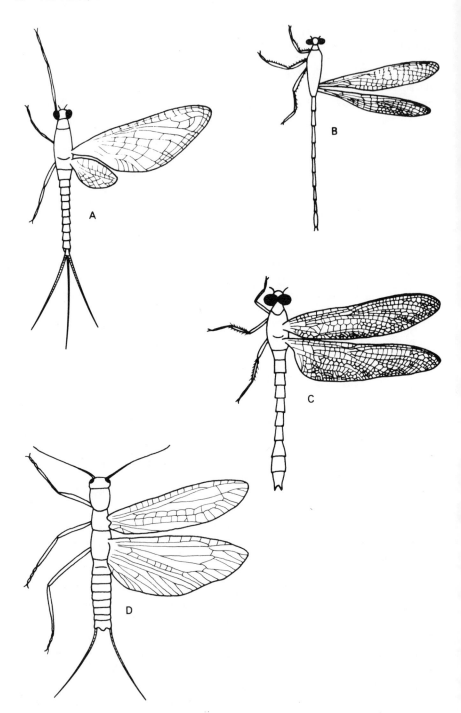

Figure 2.3 *Ephemeroptera, Odonata and Plecoptera* **A** Ephemeroptera (mayflies) **B** Odonata: Zygoptera (damsel-flies) **C** Odonata: Anisoptera (dragonflies) **D** Plecoptera (stoneflies)

The illustrated account of the Pterygota, then, should be taken for what it is; a quick survey, full of sweeping statements, that provides reference points for what follows.

The EPHEMEROPTERA or mayflies (Figure 2.3). The eyes are large, the antennae and mouthparts minute in the adult stage. The wings are membranous, with many cross veins, and are held vertically when at rest; the hind-wings are usually small. The cerci are long and there is usually a long median filament from the last abdominal segment. The nymphs are aquatic (Figure 1.8C page 23) and towards the end of nymphal life a form known as the sub-imago is produced; it resembles the adult, and can fly, but is in fact covered by a thin cuticle which is then moulted. It is the only example in the Pterygota of a moult in a quasi-adult state. The nymphal stages may last several years, the adults only a few hours.

The ODONATA or dragonflies and damsel-flies (Figure 2.3, and 4.22 page 82). An Order of insects which are adapted both in the aquatic nymphal stage and in the fast-flying adult stage to an active predacious existence (Chapter 4 page 81). The eyes and jaws are very large, the antennae small. There are two Sub-Orders, the Zygoptera or damsel-flies and the Anisoptera or dragonflies proper. Figure 2.3 brings out the principal adult differences.

The PLECOPTERA, or stoneflies (Figure 2.3), are delicate insects. The membranous wings have many cross veins and, at rest, are folded flat across the back. The hind-wing has a broad basal region, which is one of the features that link the Plecoptera with the Orthoptera. The abdomen may bear cerci. The adults feed very little; the aquatic nymphs are mostly herbivorous.

The GRYLLOBLATTODEA are a very small Order important only because the eight species are probably living fossils of the stock from which the primitive orthopteroid groups evolved (Chapter 3 page 57).

The ORTHOPTERA (Figure 2.4) are a major Order. The mouthparts are simple and suited for biting. The fore-wing is harder than the membranous hind-wing and in flight is not flapped but held out sideways like an aeroplane's wing. Many species are apterous in one or both sexes. Jumping, by means of modified hind-legs is characteristic of the Order. There are usually organs for sound production (stridulation) and reception.

The PHASMIDA are the stick-insects and leaf-insects. They display protective colouration and form: the stick-insects resemble twigs (Figure 2.4) while the leaf-insects have leaf-like protruberances on the body and legs. They have biting mouthparts and are usually apterous. Many are parthenogenetic.

The DERMAPTERA or earwigs (Figure 2.5). These have biting mouthparts and the small fore-wing is hardened to form a covering for the large hind-wing which, at rest, is much folded. The cerci are modified as pincers and used at least in some species for folding the hind-wings. Some species are apterous.

The EMBIOPTERA (Figure 2.5) are a minute order. The females are apterous. The

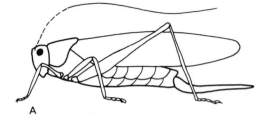

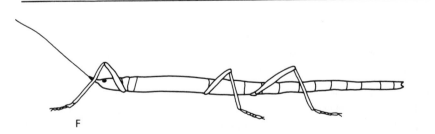

Figure 2.4 *Orthoptera and Phasmida* Orthoptera: **A** Tettigoniidae (longhorn grasshoppers or bush crickets) **B** Gryllidae (crickets) **C** Gryllotalpidae (mole crickets) **D** Tetrigidae (grouse locusts) **E** Acrididae (shorthorn grasshoppers). Phasmida: **F** a stick-insect

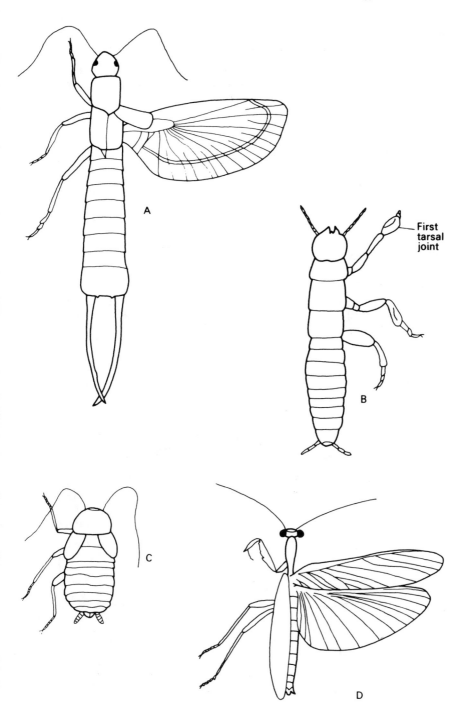

First
tarsal
joint

Figure 2.5 *Dermaptera, Embioptera and Dictyoptera* **A** Dermaptera **B** Embioptera
C Dictyoptera: Blattidae **D** Dictyoptera: Mantidae

first joint of the anterior tarsus is enlarged and contains a silk gland with which a silken tunnel is produced. The insects live in the tunnels, often gregariously.

The DICTYOPTERA or cockroaches and mantids (Figure 2.5). They have biting mouthparts and long slender antennae; the fore-wings are thicker than the hind-

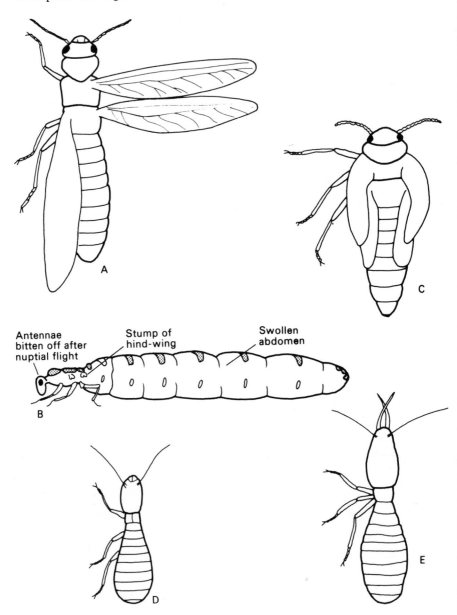

Figure 2.6 *Isoptera (termites)* **A** king (left fore-wing removed) **B** egg-laying queen **C** replacement queen **D** worker **E** soldier

wings but aptery is common. The Blattidae are the cockroaches, important in nature as scavengers and to man as nuisances rather than as pests. The Mantidae are interesting on account of their extreme carnivorous adaptations (Page 81 and Figure 4.24).

The ISOPTERA or termites (Figure 2.6). One of the most interesting and economically important Orders, with a social organization divided into several castes (Chapter 5 page 127) most of which are apterous: but where wings occur, the fore and hind-wings are similar. They have biting mouthparts.

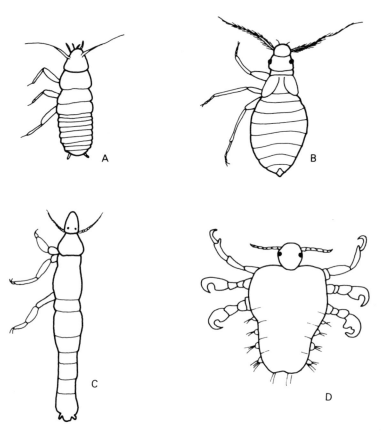

Figure 2.7 **A** Zoraptera **B** Psocoptera (book lice) **C** Mallophaga (biting lice) **D** Siphunculata (sucking lice)

The ZORAPTERA (Figure 2.7). A minute Order of minute insects, with biting mouthparts. They are gregarious; found under bark or in the soil.

The PSOCOPTERA or book-lice (Figure 2.7). Their mandibles are of the biting type; the maxillae are modified to form a long rasping organ. The body is soft. Aptery is common.

The MALLOPHAGA or biting lice (Figure 2.7), are apterous, have biting mouthparts and are ectoparasites on birds and mammals (Chapter 4 page 100 and Figure 4.41B).

The SIPHUNCULATA or sucking lice (Figure 2.7) have piercing and sucking mouthparts, and little external sign of body segmentation: highly modified for ectoparasitic life (Chapter 4 page 100, Figure 4.41A and Chapter 6 page 158).

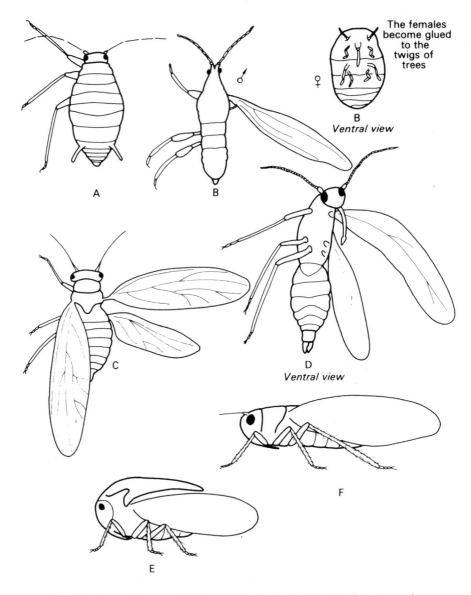

The females become glued to the twigs of trees

Figure 2.8 *Hemiptera : Homoptera* **A** Aphididae (aphids) **B** Coccidae (scale insects) **C** Psyllidae (jumping plant lice) **D** Aleyrodidae (white flies) **E** Membracidae (tree hoppers) **F** Jassidae (leaf hoppers)

The HEMIPTERA or bugs. The Order covers a diverse assembly of insects whose chief common feature is the piercing and sucking mouthparts together with their protective sheath or rostrum. The two Sub-Orders are very distinct, being often treated as separate Orders. The Homoptera (Figure 2.8) can be distinguished from the Heteroptera (Figure 2.9) on features of the wings and mouthparts. In the Homoptera the wings are folded over the abdomen in a sloping roof-like manner, whereas in the Heteroptera they are folded flat. The fore and hind-wings of the Homoptera are similar in texture, but in the Heteroptera the fore-wing is thickened over most of its area leaving a membranous region near the tip. Nearly all Homoptera hold their mouthparts close against the ventral surface of the head and thorax, while the Heteroptera hold them clear of the body.

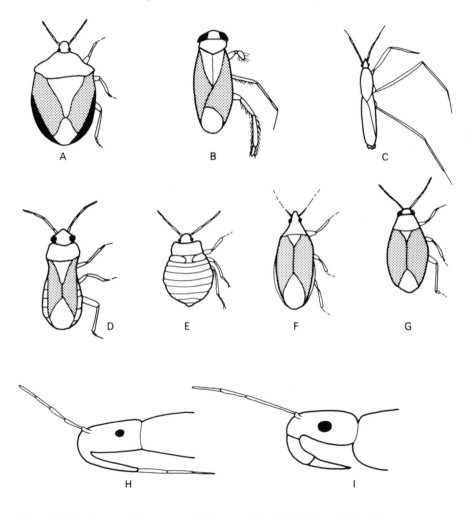

Figure 2.9 *Hemiptera : Heteroptera* **A** Pentatomidae **B** Corixidae **C** Gerridae **D** Coreidae **E** Cimicidae **F** Anthocoridae **G** Miridae **H** typical heteropteran head, in side view **I** head of reduviid to show the short stout predacious rostrum

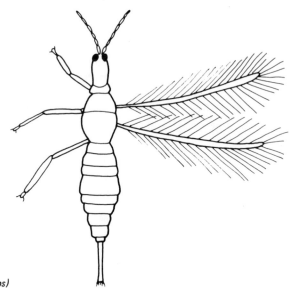

Figure 2.10 *Thysanoptera (thrips)*

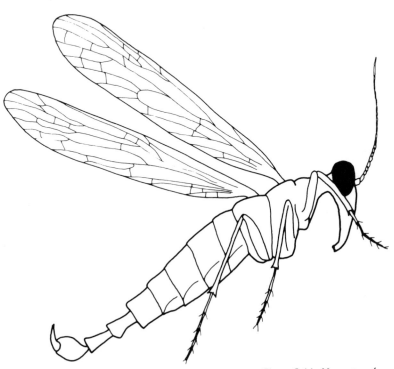

Figure 2.11 *Mecoptera (scorpion-flies)*

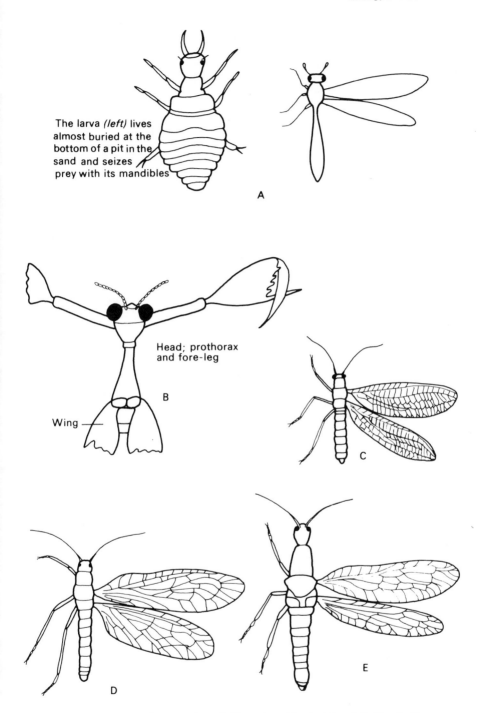

The larva *(left)* lives almost buried at the bottom of a pit in the sand and seizes prey with its mandibles

A

Head; prothorax and fore-leg

B

Wing

C

D

E

Figure 2.12 *Neuroptera :* Planipennia : **A** Myrmeleontidae (ant lions) **B** Mantispidae **C** Chrysopidae (green lacewings). Megaloptera : **D** Sialidae (alder flies) **E** Raphididae (snake flies)

The THYSANOPTERA or thrips (Figure 2.10), are an Order of very small insects with mouthparts adapted first for rasping the surface of plant tissues and then for sucking the juices. The wings are narrow and fringed, but aptery often occurs.

The subsequent Orders are all members of the Endopterygota.

The MECOPTERA or scorpion-flies (Figure 2.11), are a small Order important chiefly for the light which it sheds, largely through its fossil members, on the origin of the Endopterygota. The wings are profusely veined and the head prolonged downwards to form a beak. They have biting mouthparts.

The NEUROPTERA (Figure 2.12), have membranous wings with many veins, biting mouthparts and prominent antennae. The Order is composed of two Sub-Orders: The Megaloptera (eg Sialidae and Rhaphididae) and the Planipennia (eg the other Families shown in the illustration) are separated principally on larval features, the larvae of Megaloptera having biting mouthparts while those of the Planipennia are adapted for sucking.

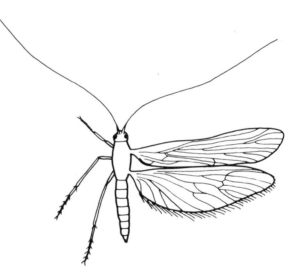

Figure 2.13 *Trichoptera (caddisflies)*

The TRICHOPTERA or caddisflies (Figure 2.13), have wings covered in hairs and sometimes, scales. Their mouthparts are reduced in the adults, which never feed. The larvae are always aquatic.

The LEPIDOPTERA or butterflies and moths, are one of the largest Orders, with wings densely clad in scales. The mouthparts are modified to form a sucking proboscis which is coiled under the head.

The DIPTERA or true flies (Figure 2.14). A vast Order, unique in having only one pair of wings, the hind pair being modified as halteres or balancing organs. They have mouthparts for sucking or piercing.

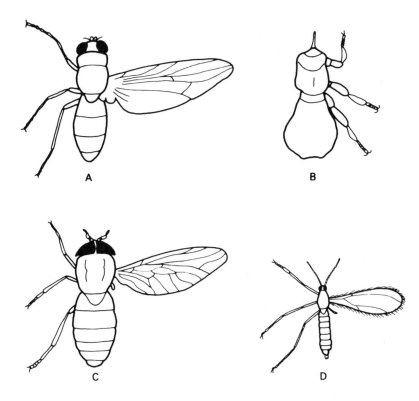

Figure 2.14 *Diptera* : Cyclorrhapha : **A** Muscidae **B** Hippoboscidae. Brachycera :
C Tabanidae. Nematocera : **D** Cecidomyidae

There are three Sub-Orders. The illustration does no more than show their chief features in terms of one representative Family from each. Differences within Sub-Orders, especially amongst the very numerous Cyclorrhapha, do not lend themselves to this kind of illustration.

The Nematocera have antennae with many segments and an elongated abdomen. Their larvae usually have well developed heads, as in mosquito larvae, or the head capsule may be partly retracted into the thorax as in leatherjackets (Figure 6.7A).

The Brachycera have antennae of three segments (the last one has external rings which make the antennae appear many-jointed), and many segments are apparent in the abdomen. The larval head capsule is partly retracted.

The Cyclorrhapha have very short antennae with a bristle, or arista, and the segments of the abdomen are telescoped so that not all are visible externally. The larva is a headless maggot. The Family Hippoboscidae includes some highly atypical forms such as the sheep ked, which is apterous and adapted to an ectoparasitic existence.

The SIPHONAPTERA or fleas (Figure 2.15), display many adaptations to ecto-parasitic life; aptery, lateral compression of the body, devices for clinging to the host, reduction of sense organs, piercing and sucking mouthparts (Chapter 4 page 98).

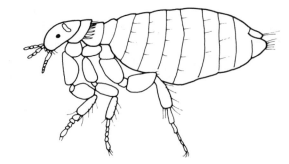

Figure 2.15 *Siphonaptera (fleas)* a dog flea

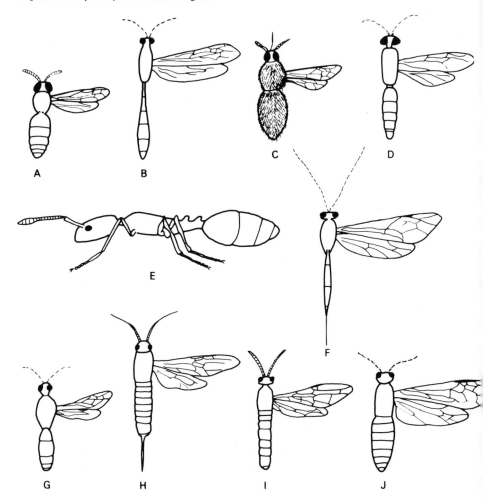

Figure 2.16 *Hymenoptera* : Apocrita : **A** a vespid **B** a sphecid **C** an apid **D** a pompilid **E** a formicid **F** an ichneumonid (a member of the Parasitica) **G** a scoliid. Symphyta: **H** Siricidae **I** Cephidae **J** Tenthredinidae

The HYMENOPTERA (Figure 2.16). A vast and highly variable Order, but easy to recognize at sight. The wings are membranous and glossy with reduced venation; fore and hind-wings are coupled by means of hooks on the hind-wings; mouthparts are adapted usually for biting but, in the highest forms, for sucking. The first segment of the abdomen is fused with the thorax, but this feature is not very evident in the Sub-Order Symphyta. The ovipositor is usually prominent and often adapted for laying eggs inside plant and animal tissues or modified as a sting. Aptery and social life occur in some forms.

The Sub-Order Symphyta has the abdomen broadly attached to the thorax, while in the Sub-Order Apocrita the anterior part of the abdomen is narrowed to form a 'wasp waist'. The wing venation of the Apocrita is reduced as compared with that of the Symphyta. The Apocrita are composed of two large groups; the Parasitica and the Aculeata. The Parasitica have ovipositors adapted for piercing.

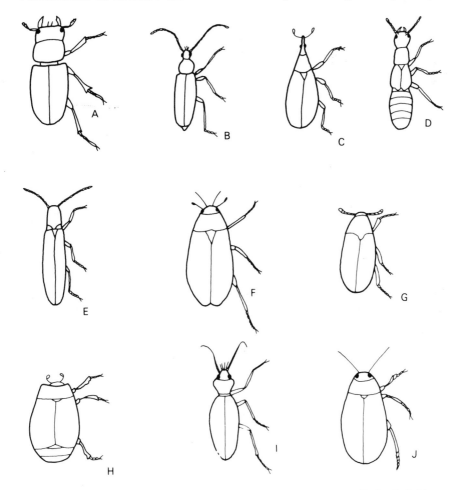

Figure 2.17 *Coleoptera* **A** lucanidae **B** Cerambycidae **C** Curculionidae **D** Staphylinidae **E** Elateridae **F** Hydrophilidae **G** Dermestidae **H** Histeridae **I** Carabidae **J** Dytiscidae

They lay their eggs in other insects thereby acting as important controls on many pest species; the Ichneumonidae are a representative Family of this group. The remainder of Figure 2.16 illustrates the Aculeata, the group in which the ovipositor is modified as a sting.

The COLEOPTERA or beetles (Figure 2.17) are the largest Order. The fore-wing is modified as an elytron, being hard and serving as a protective cover for the hind-wing. In flight the elytra are usually held out laterally like the wings of aeroplanes and take no active part in locomotion. Adult and larval mouthparts are always of the biting type.

This Order is so vast that the illustration can give but the most superficial impression of its diversity. The division into Families is based largely on features of the antennae.

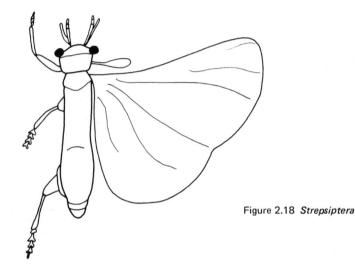

Figure 2.18 *Strepsiptera*

The STREPSIPTERA (Figures 2.18 and 4.42) are very small, highly modified insects. The females are endoparasites. The males have branched antennae and reduced fore-wings.

Chapter 3
Insect Evolution

The arthropods are polyphyletic, that is to say that the term Arthropoda includes a large number of major groups which are now known to have evolved arthropod features by different routes. An exoskeleton, jointed appendages and musculature of a generalized arthropod type are all useful features so it is not surprising that they should have been evolved many times, and the possession of them is no longer thought to denote common ancestry.

The insects, according to Manton, constitute a section of the Phylum Uniramia, one of the four phyla of 'arthropods' (Figure 3.1).

Manton's view is based primarily on a study of function, especially that of the limbs' action in walking and feeding. She shows that the ancestors of the Uniramia (arthropods with unbranched appendages) already possessed haemocoels and lobopodial rather than parapodial limbs, and that we can no longer make any

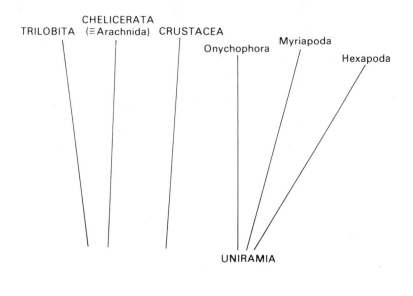

Separate Ancestors

Figure 3.1 *Arthropod groups on the basis of jaws and trunk limbs* (slightly adapted from Manton)

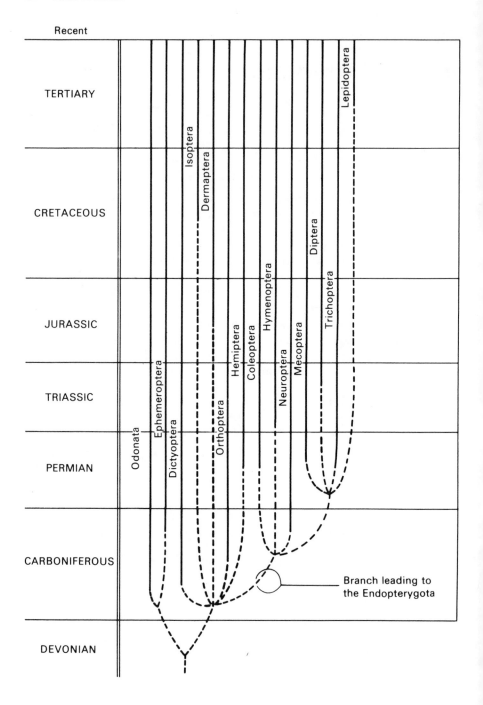

Figure 3.2 *Evolutionary relationships of the major insect orders* (dotted lines indicate likely relationships)

assumptions about the evolution of arthropods from annelid ancestors. The most that can be suggested is their evolution from ancestors of the annelids; indeed the only positive similarity between annelids and arthropods is that they are metamercally segmented.[1]

The earliest fossil records of insects are from the Carboniferous. They include forms adapted to feeding on living plant material, scavengers and carnivores. By the middle Permian most of the major Orders existed but some of the more specialized ones (Diptera, Hymenoptera and Lepidoptera) arose later. A few Orders, chiefly those which are parasitic on homiothermic vertebrates, are of recent origin (Figure 3.2).

The oldest fossils are grouped in the Order Palaeodictyoptera which is omitted from Figure 3.2 because its relationship to the existing Orders is obscure. Figure 3.3 shows many of its features. These features, with modifications, are to be found in the more primitive Orders of living winged insects (Ephemeroptera, Odonata, Grylloblattodea, Orthoptera, Dictyoptera) with the exception of the lateral outgrowths of the prothorax and the abdominal segments. It is possible that wings may have originated as lateral outgrowths on some or all of the body segments. Even small flat outgrowths would presumably have given the body some support for a glide after a small jump or a drop, and the feature may have been retained since it conferred the advantage of improved locomotion. This is pure speculation since the earliest fossils of winged insects have fully developed wings, not unlike those of dragonflies, but it is a reasonable supposition by analogy with the use which some arboreal vertebrates make of lateral flaps. We know nothing for certain about the origin of flight, nor indeed about the way in which the lateral outgrowths eventually became articulated with the thorax instead of being continuous with it. The course of evolution of indirect as opposed to direct flight

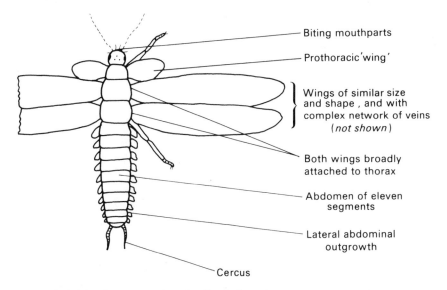

Figure 3.3 *A Paleodictyopteran (a carboniferous insect)*

muscles is also a mystery. On the assumption that wings originated from lateral flaps it seems reasonable that, for the sake of stability, the thoracic rather than the abdominal ones should have been used. It is less obvious why the prothoracic segment should have been discarded as a wing-bearer for on mechanical grounds it should have been as suitable as the others, although being smaller, with less musculature available for wing movement, may have disqualified it. Three pairs of wings would perhaps have created too great a co-ordination problem.

Insect evolution is closely correlated with that of the potential food supply. The Carboniferous forest floor supplied plentiful debris for litter-feeders and there were probably accumulations of spores, but we have no direct evidence of insect—plant inter-relationships at this stage. The 'cockroach' type of mouthparts was suited to litter-feeding and the Dictyoptera would seem to be of very great antiquity, as are the related Orthoptera. Although we know nothing of the feeding habits of the Carboniferous Orthoptera it is reasonable to suppose that the lycopod flora supplied suitable shoots and leaves for a herbivorous diet. The carnivorous Odonata were plentiful — some were of great size with a wing span of over fifty centimetres, but we have no record of their nymphs — and so were the Ephemeroptera of whose nymphs there are plenty of fossils. The carnivorous Neuroptera, too, are found in the early rocks.

The other major Order of Exopterygota, the Hemiptera, had to wait until the Permian. Few Carboniferous plants possessed a continuous cylinder of xylem: most had their vascular tissue set deep in the stem, under a thick cortex. That structure was not suited to the typical hemipteran method of feeding which calls for an accessible cylinder of vascular tissue close to the surface of the stem or, alternatively, for delicate leaves into which the proboscis can be thrust. The change from a predominantly pteridophyte vegetation to a predominantly gymnosperm one, which began in the late Carboniferous, favoured hemipteran evolution.

The Coleoptera with their relatively unspecialized mouthparts evolved early, as did the Hymenoptera. These hymenopterans however had biting mouthparts, like the sawflies (Figure 4.33): the nectar-sucking forms had to wait until the emergence of the advanced angiosperms in the late Cretaceous and more particularly in the Tertiary.

The five remaining major Orders, Mecoptera, Neuroptera, Trichoptera, Lepidoptera and Diptera are probably linked to the Coleoptera and Hymenoptera through the ancestors of the Mecoptera or the Neuroptera.

The Mecoptera today are a small Order of about 200 species with a world-wide distribution. The Permian contains many fossils of Mecoptera and they closely resemble the living forms. Their wing venation suggest that they may have given rise to the Neuroptera, Diptera, Trichoptera and Lepidoptera.

The Trichoptera, evolving in the Permian, would have had to rely on solid food. Their adults feed scarcely at all, having very short mouthparts which are suitable only for lapping liquids. The larvae, however, being carnivorous and aquatic were able to obtain what they needed from the aquatic fauna of small Crustacea.

Life cycles which include larvae and the feature of metamorphosis are not confined to insects: many invertebrates possess them. Larvae can be of great value to aquatic animals as a means of dispersal, especially when the adult is sessile as in the case of sea anemones, barnacles and many others or, like the sea urchins, confined to slow walking on the bottom. Parasites often depend on their larval stages for transmission.

On land larval stages do not present so many advantages, and comparatively few terrestrial animals possess them. Hardly any land animals are sessile; they disperse themselves as adults by walking or crawling. The general principle amongst aquatic invertebrates is that the larval stages being lighter, are more readily dispersed than the adults, so that often a bottom-living, slow-moving, animal may have a larva which floats near the surface and is carried by currents. Clearly none of that could apply on land. Furthermore in the majority of cases the terrestrial invertebrate is liable to desiccation and a small, delicate, larval stage would be even more vulnerable than the adult.

The only other invertebrates which can be regarded as truly land-adapted, in the sense of being able to move freely in dry air at high temperatures, are the spiders and some other Chelicerata ($\equiv$ Arachnida). Spiders do not have metamorphosis: their eggs hatch into miniature copies of the adults, and yet they exist in vast numbers in a wide variety of habitats, and are a highly successful group. Why then have the insects made such great use of larval forms? Evidently it is not for the sake of dispersal (except in some special cases associated with parasitism) because the adult insects' power of flight is quite sufficient for that.

The answer lies in the almost incredible flexibility of the ways in which insects exploit their environment. Spiders have done well for themselves, but on more limited lines than the insects. They are exclusively carnivorous, and so are cut off from directly tapping an immense supply of food. At time of food shortage their numbers dwindle. This feature is unimportant in the tropics, but in those parts of the world where the seasonal cycle is well marked it is a disadvantage. Spiders survive the inclement season by the survival of a small number of adult individuals which build the population up again when conditions improve.

Insect larval stages, then, can be seen as one of the means by which insects have become the most successful invertebrates in the sense of making the fullest use of their environment for the greatest possible time and in the most diverse ways even in the life-time of a single individual. The last point is important. A land-living adult may have an aquatic larva, the larvae of many aquatic adults come on land to pupate and herbivorous adults may have carnivorous larvae. Adults which feed on plants in one way may have larvae which do so in another. The adult may be short-lived and hardly feed at all, acting merely as a reproductive stage and leaving the feeding to the larva which probably lives in a safer environment. Most valuable of all, the pupal stage has enabled insects to perform the complicated process of transforming the larva into the adult in a safe and inconspicuous way which also serves as an excellent means of surviving the inclement season.

Not all insects, however, have a pupal stage. In the more primitive forms the egg hatches into a larva which resembles the adult in a general way, differing from it chiefly in the proportions of the various parts of the body, in not possessing wings, and, of course, in being sexually immature. In the more advanced forms the egg hatches into a larva so different from the adult that their relationship could not be deduced from their morphology. Complete restructuring is needed to produce the adult. It is for this reason that the more advanced insects need the pupal stage which, in addition, confers ecological advantages.

The student who is not familiar with the classification and general evolutionary pattern of insects will find it useful at this stage to refer back to the beginning of Chapter 2. The ancestors of the most primitive insects, the Apterygota, never possessed wings. In these insects the larval stages bear close resemblance to the adults, differing from them only in small details.

The winged insects fall readily into two great groups, with hardly any overlap. In the Exopterygota the larval stages (often called nymphs) develop wings from wing-pads which are visible externally, whereas in the Endopterygota the larvae exhibit no trace of wings. In the pupa wings develop from the sudden multiplication of undifferentiated cells localized in regions known as imaginal discs. Not only wings are formed in that way but most of the larval tissues are broken down and the adult ones formed each by proliferation of the appropriate disc. The pupa, therefore, is anything but a resting stage: it is a time of intense physiological activity. So great is this distinction between the two types of development that it suggests a dichotomy in the ancestry of insects. Figure 3.2 suggests, very speculatively, the stage at which the Endopterygota diverged.

There are good reasons for believing that the Endopterygota evolved from exopterygotes and are not a separate line stemming from still more distant non-insectan ancestors. In the absence of fossil links we have to look for circumstantial evidence. We find some in the occasional abnormal form of the meal worm (Figure 3.4) which bears external wing rudiments on each of the two wing-bearing thoracic segments. This phenomenon may imply that the larvae of the ancestors of the group had external wing rudiments before entering the pupal stage, in other words that a winged prepupal stage existed. Again, in some Exopterygota (the Thysanoptera and some Hemiptera) a stage resembling the

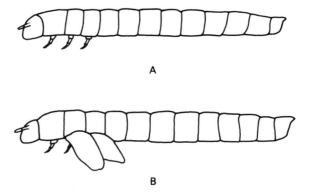

A

B

Figure 3.4 *A mealworm — larva of the beetle* Tenebrio molitor **A** Normal form **B** Mutant form in which wing rudiments appear externally

endopterygote pupa exists. The early larval stages of these exopterygotes do not resemble the adults, the wing rudiments form only in the later stages, where they grow internally, under the larval cuticle. The last of these stages is inactive; to all intents and purposes a pupa. There are, therefore, grounds for believing that the distinction between the exo- and endopterygote condition is not absolute, and that the one gave rise to the other. The reason for the small number of links is, no doubt, that the full endopterygote condition has proved highly successful, for whereas the larvae of most Exopterygota not only resemble the adults but also tend to lead a similar existence (with the exception of the aquatic larvae) the same is not true of the Endopterygota. By having two modes of life the endopterygotes greatly extend the use which they make of available resources of food and habitat.

When we speak of insect evolution we must think in terms of the whole insect, not merely of its adult or larval life. There is, though, a sense in which we can use the term 'larval evolution' to denote the change in function, and therefore in structure, of the larval stages. Figure 3.5 shows in highly simplified fashion the main types of endopterygote larvae. It will be seen that much of the chart is concerned with the Coleoptera which is not only an old Order but the one which has succeeded best of all in adapting itself to a wide variety of ways of life. The manner in which the adults of the Order have radiated will be discussed in the next chapter; suffice it to say that the Order ranges from relatively unspecialized members such as the Carabidae and Staphylinidae (Figure 2.17), which lead a generalized ground-dwelling existence as adults, to forms which lead highly specialized modes of life. The numbering of Figure 3.5 shows a gradually increasing scale of specialization, though not an evolutionary series, the Carabidae being considered on normal taxonomic grounds to be the most primitive beetles.

The larvae at the beginning of the series are active animals with obvious insect-like features apart from the absence of wings. In fact they bear a superficial resemblance to the adults of some of the Apterygota (Figure 2.2). Then there is a gradual loss of the features which are associated with active life; legs become reduced and are finally lost in the weevils, while eyes and antennae are similarly reduced. The difference between larva and adult becomes greater with increasing evolutionary advance.

A similar pattern emerges when we examine the larvae of the other major Orders. The primitive lepidopteran larva is not a caterpillar but a much more active animal with long antennae and legs on nearly all its abdominal segments, whereas the caterpillar which is characteristic of most Lepidoptera has pro-legs on only some segments and the sense organs are much reduced. In the Hymenoptera the primitive sawfly has a larva very similar to that of the caterpillar whilst the larvae of the advanced social wasps and bees, in relation to their passive existence, have no appendages and only slight cephalization.

In the Diptera even the primitive forms are apodous, but short antennae are present and so are biting mandibles, a primitive feature which is never found in adult Diptera. There are spiracles on most segments. The highly evolved Cyclorrhapha, however, have an even more reduced larva, the maggot, which

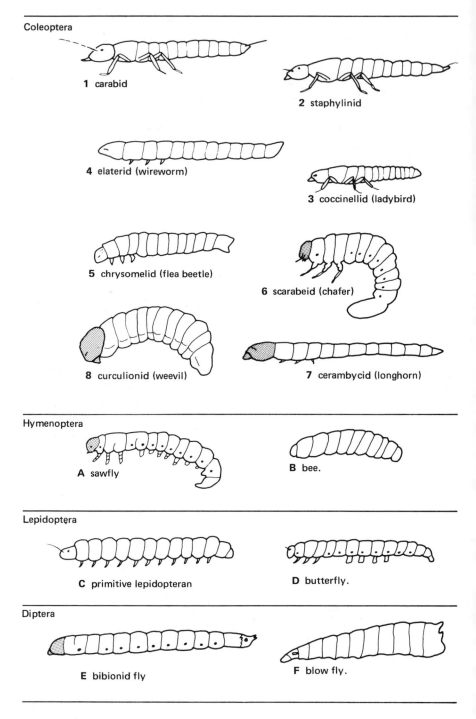

Figure 3.5 *Some endopterygote larval types.*

possesses no antennae at all; its mouthparts are secondary structures not related to paired appendages, and spiracles are confined to the first and last segments. The cyclorrhaphan maggot and adult show the greatest degree of difference between any larva and adult insect, and in this connection it is worth nothing that the pupa of the Cyclorrhapha is exceptional in being protected by the hard puparium which is formed from the cuticle of the final larval stage. In order to emerge from the hard casing the adult exerts blood pressure against its sides, and gradually cracks it open. That is true of the lower members of the Cyclorrhapha (eg hover-flies), but the most advanced ones (house-flies and blow flies) have evolved a final sophistication, the ptilinum, a sac-like ingrowth at the front surface of the head. When blood pressure distends this sac, and thrusts it out between two of the plates of the head capsule, the anterior end of the puparium is cracked open. The newly-emerged adult has its ptilinum projecting out of the front of its head but soon a small muscle pulls the ptilinum back inside and the slit in the head capsule fuses up. Neither the ptilinum nor its muscle serve any further function: they represent a special adaptation to meeting the needs of a very advanced form of life on land.

Referring again to Figure 3.5 it will be seen that the typical lepidopteran caterpillar is resembled not only by the primitive hymenopteran larva but to a large extent by that of the flea beetle as well. They all lead similar lives, feeding on plant tissues with their biting jaws. Often larvae of this type in all three Orders live *in* the tissues, as stem-borers or leaf-miners. For that kind of life a caterpillar form is well suited, and it could be argued that the similarity of larval forms in the various endopterygote Orders, and the similar trends in larval form (from the active to the passive), are the result of similar life styles favouring similar mor-phological adaptations — in other words, of convergence. The opposite view is that these similarities stem from some phylogenetic relationship. The latter interpretation is the more probable because the morphological similarities are really very strong: it is difficult to see why convergence should lead to more than superficial resemblances, and it is easier to believe in the common ancestry of the Endopterygota.

Reference

1. MANTON, S.M. (1973). Arthropod phylogeny. *J. Zool., Lond.* **171**, 111–130.

Chapter 4
Adaptive Radiation

In large groups of organisms, which consist of many species, some members have adapted the group's general features in ways that have enabled them to occupy many different ecological niches. As a rule the larger the group the greater the variety of the adaptations. The phenomenon is well seen in the placental mammals whose members have spread as herbivores and as carnivores, both small and large, to such different environments as plains, forest, tundra and desert. Bats have overcome the problem of flight. Others have become adapted in various degrees to aquatic life, and some to burrowing in the soil. In all their ecological niches, they compete successfully with members of lower groups but are less in competition with other placentals than if they had not radiated. In doing this the placentals have largely paralleled the adaptive radiation which the reptiles too, in their day, exhibited to a high degree.

The terms adaptive radiation and adaptation are often used indiscriminately; to try and sharpen their meaning is not mere pedantry. Adaptation is a *process*, whose end-product may be adaptive radiation. Adaptation is a phenomenon which occurs in individual members of a population in a given situation: it need not necessarily lead to any striking changes. If, however, in response to a sustained environmental demand the adaptive trend continues a long way in a particular direction the individuals concerned may develop extreme specializations which make them eminently suited to a particular way of life and not to any other. If that process has occurred frequently amongst members of a group we may claim that the *group* displays adaptive radiation. The point is that whales and bats are indisputably mammals in spite of extreme superficial differences: they are not fish and birds.

Insects, being a very large group, display adaptive radiation to a high degree. The cuticle has proved capable of almost infinite modification. The small size of insects has enabled them to adapt to many microenvironments denied to larger animals. Even more important has been their mode of development: many insects exist in quite different ecological niches at the larval and adult stages. Their high reproductive rate, in itself a reflection of their small size, has led to rapid evolution. So striking are the modifications that adaptive radiation can be shown not only in the Class as a whole but even within several of the Orders, especially in the largest one, the Coleoptera.

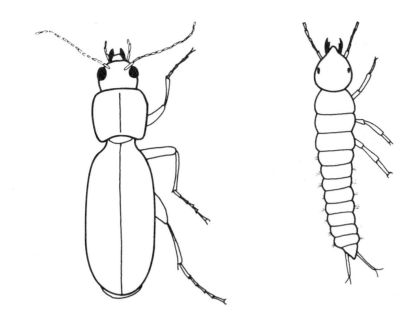

Figure 4.1 *Carabid beetle and larva*

General Adaptations in the Coleoptera

Let us consider a relatively unspecialized form, a ground-beetle (Figure 4.1). Both adult and larva are adapted for an active existence as predators on the ground. The larva will spend much of its time actually in the soil or in leaf litter where it will eventually pupate. The adult's eyes are large and mounted in a prominent position to give a good field of view: even the larva possesses eyes, which is by no means always the case in insects. The long legs permit fast running and the long antennae serve to sample the environment ahead. Both adult and larval jaws are of the biting type which is characteristic of predators.

We are not suggesting that the Family Carabidae represent the ancestral beetles but just a relatively unspecialized present-day type. The explanation which follows is intended to illustrate the range of modifications, but not to imply relationships.

Figure 4.2 shows the range of adaptation amongst the beetles: almost every ecological niche is occupied but for the sea.

The least profound adaptation is found in the Cicindelidae, the tiger beetles. They have pushed the carabid habit to its fullest extent as shown in Figure 4.3. The extreme narrowness of the tibia and tarsus demonstrates what can be done with the basic insect form: it would not be possible to reduce the diameter of a mammalian limb to so great an extent. The most delicate-limbed antelope has limbs that are relatively thicker than a tiger beetle's. The tubular nature of the limbs means that they can support a much greater weight without buckling than would mammalian limbs of the same external diameter. Since the tube can be thin-walled there is room for sufficient musculature inside it, whereas an endoskeleton would leave little room for muscles. The advantage of having a long thin limb is its lightness, so

Figure 4.2 *Adaptive radiation in the Coleoptera*

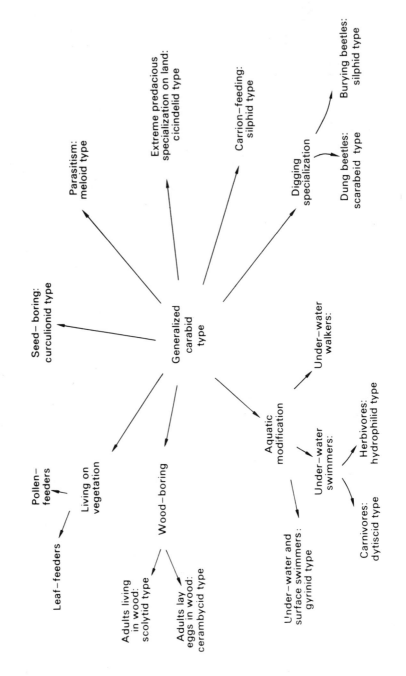

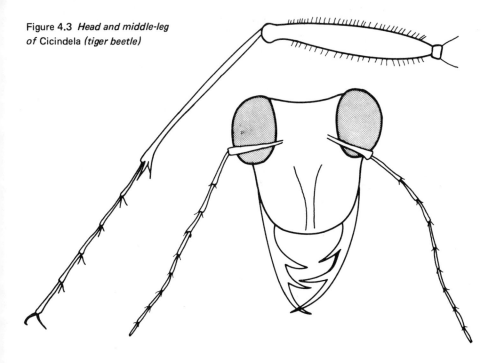

Figure 4.3 *Head and middle-leg
of* Cicindela *(tiger beetle)*

that a long stride can be achieved without having to move a heavy distal portion of
the limb which would produce such a moment about its base as to call for musculature of enormous size and weight. A thick leg when swung as in Figure 4.4 would set
up a very large moment at X.

When an insect moves it lifts a leg, swings it forward and puts it down. It then
pushes the leg against the ground. In combination with the action of the other legs
the body is thereby caused to move forward. The muscles which make the leg swing
forward and push back are called promotors and remotors respectively. They are
attached to the anterior and posterior margins of the coxa and have their origin on
the dorsal exoskeleton (Figure 4.5).

Let us suppose that these muscles are capable of releasing a certain amount of
energy.

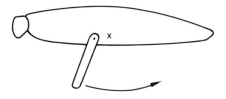

Figure 4.4

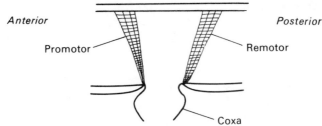

Anterior   *Posterior*

Promotor   Remotor

Coxa

Figure 4.5

In order that the body may cover a horizontal distance *l* at velocity *v* the leg must be swung forward through the angle θ with the angular velocity ω. The mass of the leg resists this motion. The resistance can be expressed by the moment of inertia *I*.

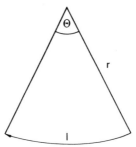

Figure 4.6

The energy needed for this linear displacement is $\frac{1}{2} I \omega^2$.
A longer leg, r_1, will achieve the same horizontal distance in the same time using a *smaller* swing, θ_1.

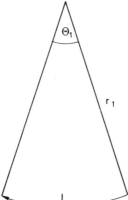

Figure 4.7

Now the angular velocity can be *lower*, ω_1, because the tip of the leg travels through a smaller angle in the same time. Less energy is therefore needed, namely $\frac{1}{2} I \omega_1^2$.
The energy saved in this way can be used to swing the leg *more frequently*, covering more ground so that the insect as a whole moves faster.

The longer leg will of course, have a greater mass and so a greater moment of inertia. The moment of inertia of a uniform rod or tube, of mass m and length r, about one end is expressed as:

$$I = \tfrac{1}{3} m\, r^2$$

Since r increases as the square of the linear dimension it becomes particularly important to keep m small — whence the value of a light leg, namely a slender one with an exoskeleton.

The tubular leg has a further advantage in not bending as readily under the body's weight as would a solid one made of the same quantity of skeletal material.

Once the leg has been lifted and moved forward it is forced back against the ground in order to push the body forward with velocity v, and energy is needed once more.

$$
\begin{aligned}
\text{The kinetic energy of the leg is} \; &= \tfrac{1}{2} I\, \omega^2 \\
&= \tfrac{1}{2} \times \tfrac{1}{3} m\, r^2\, \omega^2 \\
&= \tfrac{1}{6} m\, r^2\, v^2/r^2 \\
&= \tfrac{1}{6} m\, v^2
\end{aligned}
$$

NOTE:

It is possible to express ω as $\dfrac{v}{r}$ because

$$\theta = \frac{1}{r}$$

$$\frac{\theta}{t} = \frac{1}{rt}$$

$$\omega = \frac{v}{r}$$

Not only then is it important to keep the mass of the leg small, but it becomes more important the faster the animal has to move.

In view of its predacious and running adaptations a tiger beetle could be said to combine the attributes of the tiger with those of a racehorse: the nearest mammalian equivalent is probably the cheetah. Cicindelids are characteristic of the heathland fauna: their adaptations are useful in a sparsely populated environment where prey has to be pursued. Figure 4.8 contrasts the stance of a tiger beetle with that of a slow moving flour beetle which in nature feeds on debris.

Some beetles are scavengers. The Silphidae include members which feed on carrion. Their jaws may resemble those of ground-beetles, but the legs are not cursorial (Figure 4.9). The carrion-beetle illustrated has a mobile head with very powerful jaws. Carrion-beetles play an important part at the beginning of the disintegration of corpses: the tibial spines probably give the beetles added purchase when they wrestle with tough tissues, the strong jaws are needed to break fibres and, when mounted on a highly mobile head form excellent tools for 'worrying' the

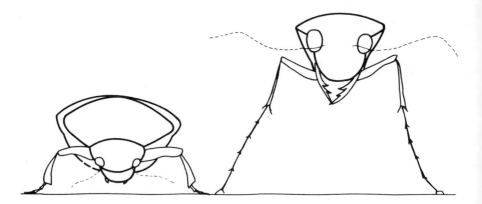

Figure 4.8 *Stance of* Tenebrio *and of* Cicindela *as seen from the front* (fore-legs only shown)

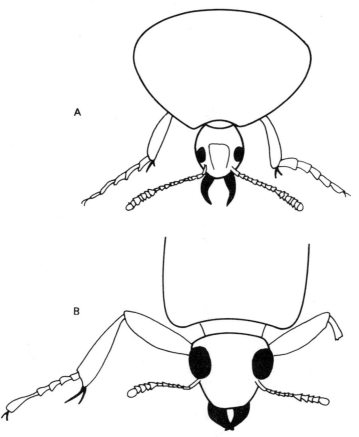

Figure 4.9 *View of two silphid beetles seen in each case from the front and slightly from above* (jaws only are shown, other mouthparts are omitted) **A** carrion-beetle **B** burying-beetle

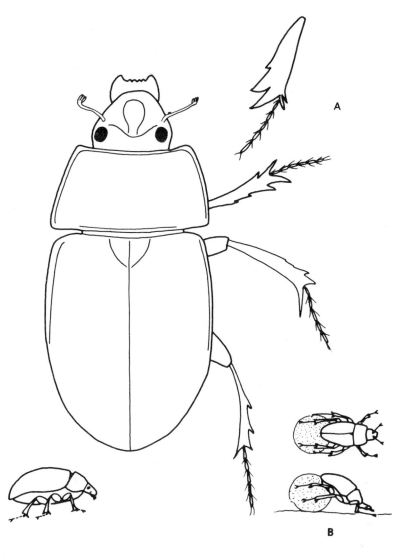

Figure 4.10 *A dung-beetle (Scarabeidae)* **A** Front view of right tibia and tarsus
B Side and top views of beetle rolling its ball of dung

carrion. Later stages of physical disintegration can, of course, be carried out by
smaller insects, including beetles, with less powerful jaws, which tackle the softer
tissues.

The burying-beetles shift soil from under carcasses with their strong legs and
blunt heads so that the bodies sink into the ground whereupon the beetles lay their
eggs in them.

The dung-beetles (Figure 4.10) contribute to the breakdown of dung. They
break off pieces of fresh dung from a pad and roll them into balls which are then
taken below ground into previously excavated pits or tunnels where an egg is laid in

each ball. In that way the beetles perform a valuable ecological function (Chapter 6 page 144). When they walk the ungainly beetles' weight is carried on the distal ends of the massive tibiae and the long tarsi serve no useful function, but when they are handling the ball of dung they display great agility. The fore-legs are kept on the ground and the ball is moulded and rolled by the middle and hind-legs which straddle it. By extending the long, strongly-clawed tarsi a good handling grip is obtained, and the breadth of the body enables the legs to gain purchase all round the ball.

Adaptation to aquatic life in the beetles

This is a profound change for a group which evolved on land; it is a secondary adaptation. The problems which faced the primitive aquatic colonizers of the land were solved by exploiting certain pre-adaptations such as the possession of a hard body cover and skeletal locomotory appendages. The terrestrial insect body had presumably been perfected before the start of secondary adaptation to aquatic life since the Order which possesses most *adult* aquatic members (apart from the Coleoptera) is the highly evolved Heteroptera. Indeed, as we have seen, the earliest known fossil insects were winged.

It is worth pointing out that the insects have, in one sense managed their secondary adaptation better than have most vertebrates since even the best adapted aquatic insects can still *fly,* although of course many are almost helpless on the ground.

The principal problems to be overcome in returning to the water are those of respiration and locomotion. Insects are fortunate in that whilst their tracheal system is a highly specialized adaptation for breathing air it can be modified quite easily for underwater breathing.

Most insects have their spiracles in a lateral position, as do the Orthoptera (Figure 4.11). Terrestrial beetles, however, typically have theirs on the upper side of the abdomen under the wings and elytra. The arrangement assumes great value as an adaptation to aquatic life when the arched elytra enclose a volume of air into which the spiracles open. All that is then necessary is for the edges of the elytra to fit closely against the abdomen to enable the beetle to retain enough atmospheric air for breathing under water. Strictly speaking a seal should be unnecessary (since the curved elytra hold the air against the abdomen as under a capsized boat) while the beetle is swimming upright and horizontally, but as soon as it tilts air would escape. In fact the seal is not absolutely air-tight, as we shall see when we discuss the action of the physical gill, so when the beetle needs to replenish its air supply it rises to the surface, tilts its head downwards, breaks the surface with the tip of its abdomen and raises its elytra sufficiently to admit a fresh supply of air.

The volume of air held under the wings is large because the beetles tend to have broader abdomens than do other insects, and the streamlining which aquatic beetles have evolved further enhances this effect (Figure 4.12).

It has been shown that many of the smaller dytiscid beetles use their sub-elytral air stores as physical gills, which enables them to remain submerged for far longer than would be the case were the store to act purely as a reserve of air. The air

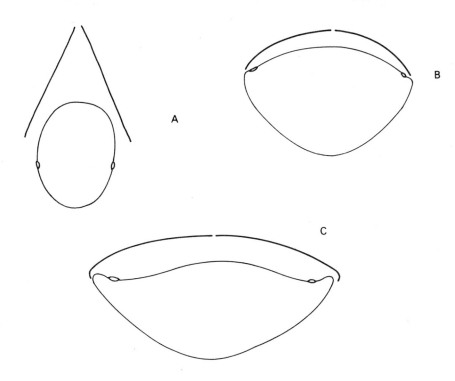

Figure 4.11 *Comparison of wing case (fore-wing) and spiracular aperture seen in a transverse section of the abdomen* **A** a typical orthopteran **B** a cicindelid beetle **C** *Dytiscus*

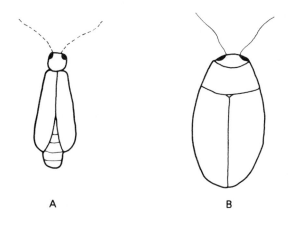

Figure 4.12 *Terrestrial and aquatic beetles compared* (legs omitted) **A** a cantharid beetle — terrestrial **B** a dytiscid beetle — aquatic

1 The insect's air store as it is about to submerge.

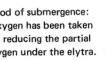

2 After a period of submergence: Much of the oxygen has been taken into the tissues reducing the partial pressure of oxygen under the elytra. Some oxygen enters from the water into the air bubble; some nitrogen, now at a higher partial pressure, passes from the bubble to the water. The bubble has become smaller.

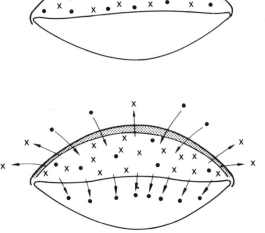

3 Towards the end of submergence: The events described in **2** above have further reduced the size of the bubble..

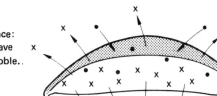

4 As the insect is about to rise: The size of the bubble no longer permits entry of sufficient oxygen to meet the insect's requirements.

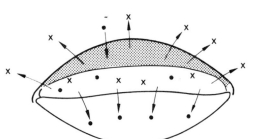

- Oxygen molecules
x Nitrogen molecules

Figure 4.13 *The physical gill*

bubble covers the spiracles and is in contact with the water. When the beetle dives air is taken into the tracheal system from the bubble and oxygen is extracted from it just as in terrestrial respiration. When much of the oxygen in the bubble has been extracted its partial pressure is lowered. Consequently dissolved oxygen enters the bubble from the surrounding water, thereby reducing the net rate at which the bubble loses oxygen. This process could continue for a long time but for the gradual reduction in the volume of the bubble as a result of loss of nitrogen from it, for as the oxygen content drops the partial pressure of the nitrogen rises and the gas tends to escape, albeit at a lower rate than that at which oxygen enters. The beetle is forced to surface when the surface area of the bubble becomes too small to allow enough oxygen to enter it from the water — when, that is to say, the action of the physical gill has broken down.

Figure 4.13 shows very diagrammatically, some aspects of this process. For convenience the entire sub-elytral space has been considered as the initial bubble, and the exchange of gases between the bubble and the water is shown as occurring across the elytra, which of course is not the case.

The action of the nitrogen in the physical gill is purely passive, it serves as a medium in which oxygen can be carried.

Hydrophilid beetles carry air down from the surface trapped in water-repellent hairs on the underside of the thorax and abdomen. The main respiratory openings are the thoracic spiracles, which are ventral, and in many cases the thoracic air bubble acts as a physical gill. The air store is renewed by the beetle approaching the surface, rolling slightly to one side and pushing the antenna of that side through the water surface. The antenna is clad in water-repellent hairs which provide a channel through which air passes to the thoracic store.

Compared with the respiratory modifications those for locomotion are relatively simple; they usually consist of converting the hind-leg into an oar. The hind-leg of *Dytiscus* is lengthened, fringed with hairs, the tarsi as well as the tibiae are flattened and the terminal claws are vestigial (Figure 4.14). The stiff hairs greatly increase the area of the leg which thrusts against the water on the power stroke, whilst on the

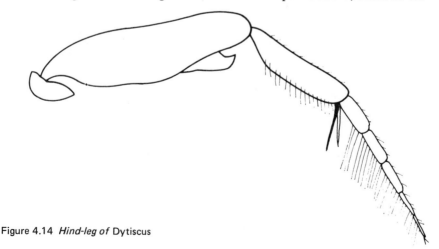

Figure 4.14 *Hind-leg of* Dytiscus

return stroke they fold back so as to reduce the resistance. The tarsus too twists so as to present the narrow edge to the water on the return stroke. The middle-leg is only slightly oar-like, and the fore-leg is not modified for swimming at all though in the male it has a large gripping pad for holding the female in copulation. The hind-leg of the actively swimming hydrophilids shows similar modifications, but the whirligig beetles (Gyrinidae), which swim fast on the surface, are very different. The fore-leg is unmodified except that, being the insect's only prehensile organ, it is

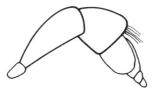

Figure 4.15 *Left hind-leg of* Gyrinus *seen from the underside*

rather longer than a typical fore-leg. The middle and hind-legs (Figure 4.15) are greatly expanded and flattened although they are so short as to be invisible from above. Again, hairs increase the area. The whole leg acts as a fan, unfolding for the power stroke as in the illustration and folding up for the return stroke.

The dytiscids have evolved a further physiological adaptation to swimming. Most insects move their legs in the sequence illustrated in Figure 4.16 so that the body follows a zig-zag track. This action was carried over into the aquatic habitat and the Hydrophilidae still exhibit it, their hind-legs thrusting backwards alternately. The Dytiscidae, however, have achieved synchronization of the hind-legs so that they thrust in unison and the beetle swims in a straight line which presumably is a desirable feature in an aquatic predator. The Hydrophilidae are herbivorous and include many members whose aquatic adaptation is relatively slight — most are underwater walkers and not swimmers at all — so that evolutionary adaptation has progressed less far.

Before leaving the topic of aquatic adaptations we shall consider a special case of modified sense organs. In the Gyrinidae the antennae are reduced but the eyes are large (Figure 4.17). In addition the eyes are divided into an upper and a lower portion on each side. It is usually thought, though experimental evidence is lacking, that divided eyes are a means of giving the insect vision simultaneously above and below water-level. The facets of the lower portion are smaller than those of the upper portion, which should produce sharp definition rather than vision over a wide field below water, which may be correlated with the gyrinids' carnivorous habit.

Adaptations to burrowing in the beetles

Many beetles burrow to various extents, either bodily as adults (usually as part of their reproductive behaviour) or by boring holes prior to oviposition: many more burrow as larvae.

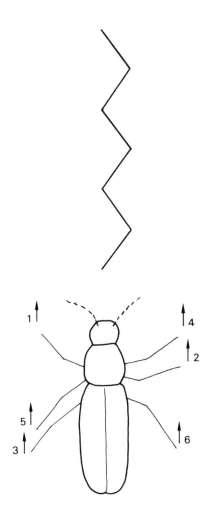

Figure 4.16 *To show the usual sequence of leg movement in insects*

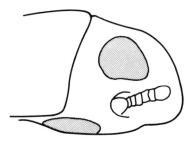

Figure 4.17 *Head of* Gyrinus *seen from the right side*

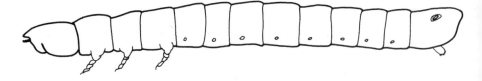

Figure 4.18 *A wireworm, the larva of a click-beetle*

Most larvae tend to be 'long and thin' and need little in the way of modifications. Wireworms, the larvae of click-beetles (Elateridae), burrow in soil and feed on roots (Figure 4.18); many are agricultural pests (page 168). For this purpose a fairly simple body plan with pointed head and short strong legs is very suitable. It can be contrasted with the form of the carabid larva's body (Figure 4.1) which is adapted for fast walking. Whilst both types of larvae are to be found in soil that of the ground-beetle uses existing crevices and moves through loose soil, but the wireworm is a true burrower. The highly motile larvae of many water-beetles pupate in damp soil near the water's edge: they do not need sophisticated burrowing adaptations either, because they burrow into a soft substratum.

Similarly larvae which bore in wood need little in the way of adaptation: stout mandibles and the almost total absence of legs are characteristic (Figure 3.5: 7) whilst the shape of the body may be adapted to the type of material to be bored — a circular cross section for boring in wood and a more flattened one for boring between the wood and the bark.

If larvae burrow in wood it is because the eggs have been laid there, as in the longhorn beetles (Cerambycidae), although the female did not penetrate the wood bodily but merely pierced it with her ovipositor. In other cases adult beetles burrow into the bark and mate there, as in the bark beetles (Scolytidae). In either case the newly-emerged adults have to bore their way out. Adult bark beetles have a squat, powerfully built body with short legs and few projections (Figure 4.19): they are pests of hardwood trees and conifers (Chapter 6 page 172). Adult longhorns are less obviously adapted to boring, having long antennae and legs. Even so the body is parallel-sided. They travel shorter distances through wood than do the bark beetles and probably make use of the larval tunnels as emergence channels, so that their rather ill-adapted shape is not a disadvantage.

The most extreme adaptations to boring are found amongst the weevils

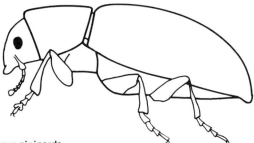

Figure 4.19 Blastophagus piniperda

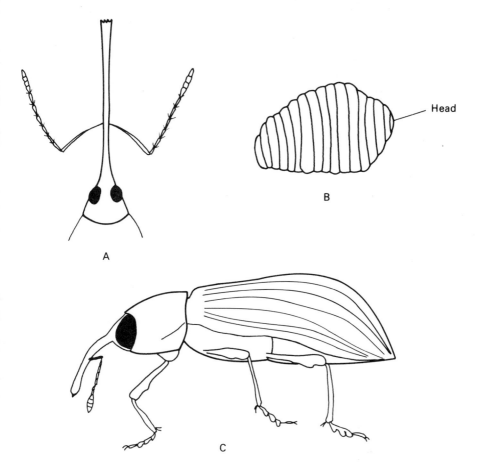

Figure 4.20 *Weevils (Curculionidae)* **A** Dorsal view of the head of *Balaninus nucum*, the nut weevil **B** a typical weevil larva **C** *Hylobius abietis,* the pine weevil

(Curculionidae). The characteristic feature of this very large Family is the elonga-
tion of the head in front of the eyes which produces a rostrum, or snout, of variable
length at the end of which are the mouthparts (Figure 4.20). Most weevils lay their
eggs in seeds or fruits, either in nature or in stored products so that they are major
pests (Chapter 6 page 176). They use their jaws to pierce the outer layer of the fruit
which may be very hard, as in stored grain, (penetrated by the grain weevils
Sitophilus spp., Chapter 6) or softer as in hazel which is penetrated before it is ripe
by the nut weevil *Balaninus nucum.* Even in the second case, though, the weevil has
a considerable problem to overcome. The insect is no more than 1·25 cm long so
that the jaws are correspondingly small and the fruit case, though green, is quite
hard. The rostrum gives added play to the jaws especially as the insect, by circling
around the region in which they are embedded, can use the rostrum as a lever. The
characteristic stance of weevils, with legs splayed out sideways so as to achieve a
good grip, is presumably correlated with that habit.

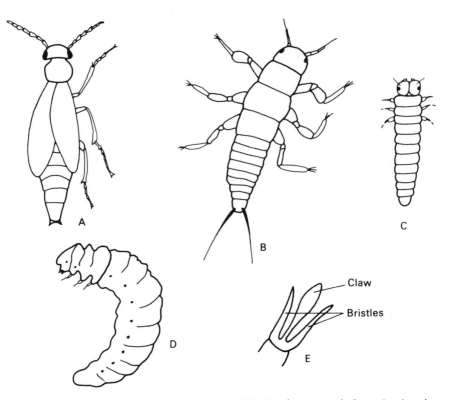

Figure 4.21 *Stages in the life cycle of an oil beetle (Meloïdae)* **A** adult (x 3 nat size, legs shown on right side only) **B** Triungulin larva (x 50 nat size, jaws not shown) **C** early and **D** late second stage larvae (x 20 nat size) **E** tip of a leg

Finally we shall consider a life style which, though widespread amongst insects is rare amongst the beetles, namely parasitism. It is a final compelling demonstration of the principle of adaptive radiation: there is scarcely anything the beetles have not tried. The oil beetles (Meloïdae) parasitize solitary bees (Figure 4.21). Large numbers of eggs are laid in the ground and the first-stage larvae into which they hatch, the triungulins, climb up vegetation and some of them arrive at flowers that are being visited by bees. The triungulins have all the features associated with active life: long legs and prominent sense organs. In addition the peculiar modification of the foot, giving them effectively three claws, enables them to grip strongly on the hairy covering of the bees. When a bee flies back to its nest in the ground it carries the beetle larvae with it. On arrival a triungulin bites its way into one of the cells and eats the egg, using its strong biting mandibles, and then consumes the food stored within the cell. It then ecdyses into a second-stage larva which resembles that of a ladybird beetle (Figure 3.5: 3) and continues to feed on the bee larva's nutritious food. Its shape changes, the legs becoming even shorter and the body flabby. After further ecdyses it becomes virtually apodous, like a weevil larva, and then pupates. There is evidently a parallel here with the life history of, say, the liver-fluke which has its active and passive larval stages. What is particularly interesting is that the various meloïd larval stages are all similar to those of other beetles, the triungulin being of the carabid type, leading through successive reduction of external features to the curculionid type. The significance of this is any one's guess; the most that can be asserted is that the Meloïdae have made the most of the genetic resources of their Order.

Adaptive radiation in other Orders

Predacious adaptations

We have considered the phenomenon in the Coleoptera which are particularly useful because of their great range of variation on the basic form. An even greater range, however, can be illustrated by taking the Class as a whole.

The beetles show good examples of predators which catch their prey on the run. Adult dragonflies (Odonata) do so in flight, whilst their aquatic nymphs too are predacious. The dragonfly swoops over its prey, often an insect resting on vegetation, with its legs dangling beneath its body like grappling-hooks. Without stopping it seizes the prey with its legs, all of which are spiny (Figure 4.22), and breaks it up with its exceptionally strong mandibles. The legs are situated just behind the head and close together to provide a formidable gripping apparatus. Vision is the essential sense for this behaviour; the eyes are huge and curved to give vision in all directions, whilst antennary sense organs are unimportant. The nymphs live near the bottom of ponds and streams partly concealed in detritus, a habit which is correlated with their short antennae. They possess large compound eyes, unlike many larval forms, and lie in wait for prey which is caught by the labium or *mask*. In the resting condition the mask is stowed away folded under the head and fore-legs, but when swung forward and unfolded it extends well in front of the head and seizes the prey by impaling it on the sharp points of the labial palps, after which the mask is folded again and, on its return action, passes the prey to the mandibles.

A parallel adaptation exists in the Diptera. The robber-flies (Brachycera: Asilidae) attack insects larger than themselves in flight, gripping them between their powerful legs, stabbing them with modified mouthparts and sucking the body fluid (Figure 4.23).

The praying mantises (Dictyoptera) capture prey amongst vegetation without pursuing it, to which end they display several adaptations (Figure 4.24). They stand on the middle and hind-legs: the fore-legs are adapted as grasping organs and are of no use in locomotion for the tarsi are vestigial. The coxa of the fore-leg is very long, the femur large, jagged and grooved along the ventral surface. The spiny tibia fits into the femoral groove when it snaps down over the prey. The effect of the elongated coxae is to thrust the femoral trap forward. Large coxae are characteristic of the other Dictyopteran family, the cockroaches, as well as of their near relatives the Orthoptera, which presumably facilitated the mantid evolution. The whole prothorax is elongated giving the mantis a better forward reach, the head is mobile, that it to say it is narrowly connected to the thorax, and triangular so that the bulging eyes have an uninterrupted field of view. The antennae in most species of man-

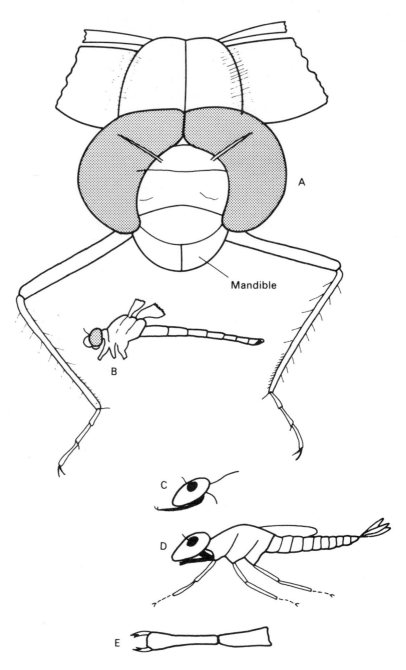

Mandible

Figure 4.22 *A dragonfly* **A** adult head and fore-legs in front view
B adult from left side **C** nymph of damsel-fly with mask
extended **D** with mask withdrawn **E** the extended mask

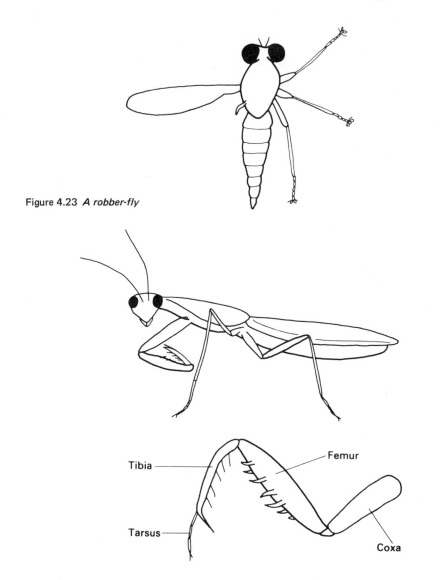

Figure 4.23 *A robber-fly*

Figure 4.24 *A praying mantis and an enlarged view of front-leg*

tis are long, which is appropriate for a sitting, as opposed to a flying, predator. A similar modification occurs in the Mantispidae (Neuroptera, Figure 2.12).

Adaptations for jumping

Several insects have a considerable power of jumping, especially the grasshoppers, some plant bugs and the springtails. So have the fleas, which will be discussed in the section on parasitism.

It is not obvious why these insects, apart from the fleas, should need to jump. Nearly all are herbivores, or scavengers, so that fast movement seems unnecessary: most such insects manage without it. With the exception of the grasshoppers' the leap is undirected, but it probably serves as an escape mechanism. For example a bush may be inhabited by a large number of leaf hoppers (Homoptera: Jassidae Figure 2.8) whose protective colouration makes them inconspicuous. If a bird lands on the bush the bugs jump off in every direction. Most fall to the ground and later fly back. This is a clear demonstration of the value of even an undirected leap as an escape mechanism, for although the bird may take one bug the remainder survive. In the case of the Jassidae the morphological adaptation is relatively slight, the hind-legs, especially the tibiae, being long.

Grasshoppers often assist their jump by flying. The principal Families of grass-hoppers are the shorthorns (Acrididae) and longhorns (Tettigoniidae) with short and long antennae respectively. The latter may be found in ground vegetation where the shorthorns live, but they often perch in shrubs and even in trees. Wingless forms often occur, especially amongst the longhorns.

Most studies of jumping have been made on locust hoppers and adults. Before it jumps the locust raises the front end of its body and bends its legs as in Figure 4.25.

Figure 4.25 *Early stages in the jump of a locust*

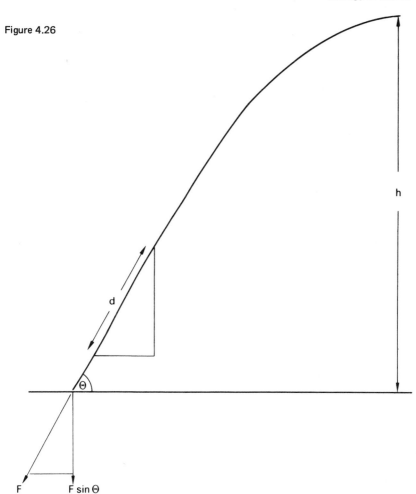

Figure 4.26

As the knee joint straightens out the body is lifted clear of the ground and moves forward. The trajectory varies, but the take-off angle usually exceeds 60°. The height of the jump decreases with the insect's weight, but increases with the take-off angle and the thrust exerted against the ground. It also increases with the distance through which the legs are extended, which can be demonstrated as follows.

Suppose the insect of Figure 4.25 begins a trajectory as shown in Figure 4.26, the take-off angle being θ and the maximum height of the jump h. The distance d along the trajectory is the linear distance by which the insect's centre of gravity has been raised by the extension of the legs before the feet left the ground – in other words while the vertical thrust was being exerted.

When the insect has reached the top of its trajectory it has gained potential energy and lost kinetic energy. If the mass of the insect is m, its vertical take-off velocity V_h and g is acceleration due to gravity,

$$\tfrac{1}{2} m V_h{}^2 = mgh$$

If the resultant force being exerted against the ground is F, its vertical component is $F \sin \theta$. If we take the force as that which acts through the centre of gravity then it has lifted the centre of gravity through the height $d \sin \theta$.

$$\text{so} \qquad F \sin \theta \times d \sin \theta = \tfrac{1}{2} mV_h^2 = mgh$$

$$\text{and} \qquad F \sin \theta = \frac{mgh}{d \sin \theta}$$

$$\text{but} \qquad mg = W$$

where W is the weight of the insect

$$\text{so} \qquad F \sin \theta = \frac{Wh}{d \sin \theta}$$

$$h = \frac{F \sin \theta \times d \sin \theta}{W}$$

From this we see that long legs, quite apart from the musculature they contain, are valuable for jumping. When we were discussing running (page 67) we found that the promotor and remotor muscles were located in the thorax, so that a tiger beetle was able to have slender legs. The jumping muscles however are in the distended femurs. The muscles are so strong that they can snap the apodèmes (internal skeletal projections) to which they are attached, as sometimes happens if the insects are held clumsily in the hand. It seems that evolution has gone to the limit in this adaptation. Many grasshoppers, however, go further, using the jump only as a highly effective prelude to flight. That applies particularly to the shorthorns, for the longhorns, although their legs are usually longer, are often poor jumpers and even poorer fliers. Figure 4.27 shows a typical longhorn beside a typical shorthorn. They are drawn as if their body lengths were equal, and it will be seen that the legs of the longhorn are relatively much longer than the shorthorn's. There is an apparent anomaly here, for one would expect the longhorns to be good jumpers. The value of long legs to the longhorns is probably for holding on to tall vegetation: indeed in that situation it would be difficult for a large insect to jump effectively in the grasshopper manner because of the absence of a firm base against which to thrust. Accordingly the thigh muscles of longhorns are usually much smaller than those of

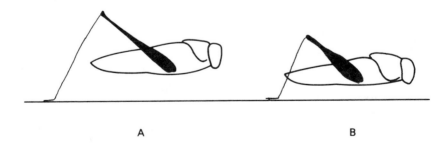

A   B

Figure 4.27 *Hind-legs in two types of grasshopper for comparison of size* **A** a longhorn
B a shorthorn

shorthorns. It is worth making the point that possession of similar structures does not invariably imply similarity of habits.

While the Orthoptera are being discussed a further extreme adaptation can be mentioned. The mole crickets (Gryllotalpidae) have modified the fore-leg for burrowing, one of the rare examples of an adult insect being profoundly modified for this purpose. They make extensive burrows, using the fore-limbs as cutting and shovelling implements (Figure 4.28).

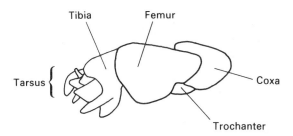

Figure 4.28 *Fore-leg of* Gryllotalpa

Adaptations for sucking

Insects of several Orders have evolved the habit of sucking the juices of plants and animals. They include those which are usually considered parasitic (eg fleas, the lice) and are discussed separately, later in this chapter, because of the very profound adaptations which they display. Most suckers, on the other hand, show little adaptation (of external features, at any rate) to the sucking habit except in their mouthparts — which reveal some of the most extreme adaptations of all As to the remainder of their bodies the suckers are either relatively unspecialized or else have the general features of their Order with the sucking modifications super-imposed.

Some Orders consist entirely, or almost entirely, of insects adapted for sucking (Hemiptera and Lepidoptera); among the Diptera suckers are in a majority while in the Hymenoptera the habit is restricted to a comparatively small but very important minority.

It follows from what has been said that the sucking habit has evolved on several separate occasions and the similar functional results have been achieved in different morphological ways. Figure 4.29 shows fairly unspecialized mouthparts in which mandibles are of the biting and crushing type, the maxilla has a long palp and in addition the galea and lacinia are fully developed. The lacinia bears strong bristles and is used in conjunction with the mandibles for breaking up the food. The mandibles and maxillae represent the first and second paired limbs. The third pair is fused to form the labium which in addition to bearing palps and the small projections, glossae and paraglossae, serves as a kind of lower lip or posterior boundary to the buccal cavity. The anterior boundary is formed by the labrum which is part of the head capsule and not strictly speaking a mouthpart (since it is not the homologue of a paired limb) but in some insects becomes a functional mouthpart. Its

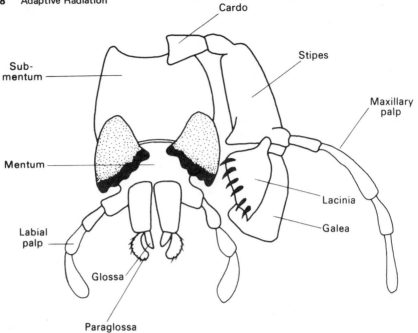

Figure 4.29 *Mouthparts of a cockroach (Dictyoptera) to show a generalized primitive arrangement* (front view, mandibles shaded, maxilla shown on left side only)

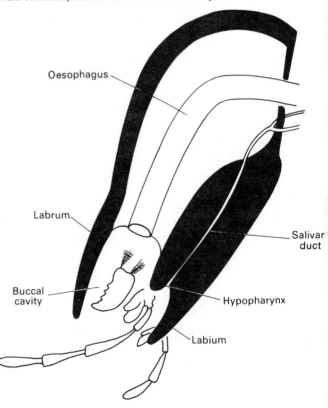

Figure 4.30 *Diagrammatic median longitudinal section through the head of a generalized insect* (The position of the mandible, maxilla and the lateral parts of the labium are shown in outline)

inner surface is called the epipharynx. Figure 4.30 shows the arrangement of the mouthparts in relation to the head capsule, and also shows the hypopharynx, a plate lying above the labium, on to which the salivary gland opens by means of a duct. The hypopharynx, too, becomes modified in some insects which are adapted for sucking.

The following table shows some of the ways in which the basic apparatus of mouthparts have been adapted for different kinds of sucking.

		Function of mouthparts	*Mouthparts involved in piercing/sucking*	*Accessory mouth parts involved*
LEPIDOPTERA		Nectar sucking	Galeae of the maxillae	
DIPTERA	Hover-Fly	Nectar sucking	Complex 'house-fly' type of sucking pad with pseudotracheae	
	Tsetse	Stabbing and blood sucking	Stabbing: Haustellum (base of labium). Sucking: Labrum and hypopharynx	
	Mosquito	Piercing and blood sucking	Piercing: Mandibles, and laciniae of maxillae. Sucking: Labrum and labium	
HYMEN-OPTERA Hive bee		Nectar sucking	Glossa of the labium	Labial palp and galeae of maxillae serve as guards
HEMIPTERA		Piercing and phloem sap sucking (and in some cases sucking animal body fluids)	Piercing and sucking: Mandibles and maxillae	Labrum and labium serve as guides

The most reduced and also the most advanced is the Lepidopteran condition. The Lepidoptera evolved late (Page 58) and fast, showing remarkable uniformity as regards their mouthparts. The most primitive Family of present-day Lepidoptera are not nectar-sucking but pollen-feeders and have many of the basic mouthparts, with mandibles adapted for biting (Figure 4.31). Two slightly more advanced Families show a trend towards the typical lepidopteran proboscis (characteristic of ninety eight per cent of the Order) in which mandibles have been completely lost, the labium is reduced to small palps and most of the maxilla has disappeared too — leaving only the elongated galeae to form the proboscis. When not in use the proboscis is stowed under the head curled in a spiral (Figure 4.32). The haemocoel of the head extends into each galea, which is linked to its neighbour by a series of hooks and interlocking spines — an extremely simple but effective mechanism.

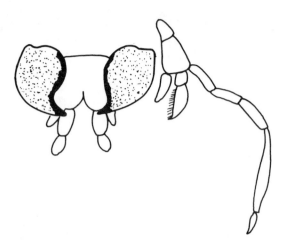

Figure 4.31 *Mouthparts of* Micropteryx, *a primitive lepidopteran* : the mandibles are of the biting type and the labium is much reduced. (The maxilla of the left side only is shown)

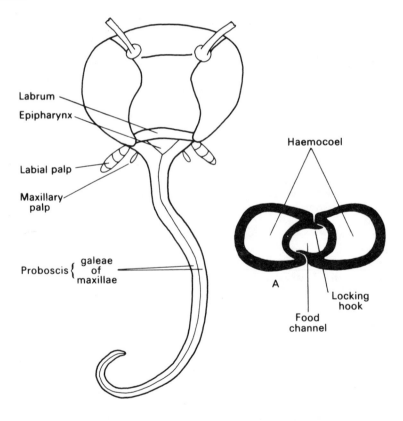

Figure 4.32 *Head and mouthparts of a butterfly* **A** Sectional diagram showing how the galeae interlock to form a channel for the nectar

Contraction of muscles in the head forces blood into the galeae, causing the proboscis to uncoil and be extended in a quite rigid manner. The median surface of each galea is concave, so that a food channel is formed between them, up which nectar can be drawn through the action of a pharyngeal pump. That the return of the proboscis to its coiled position is anything but a passive process is indicated by the large number of fine obliquely-running muscles within the galeae, accompanied by tracheae and nerves. When the head muscles relax blood flows out of the pro-

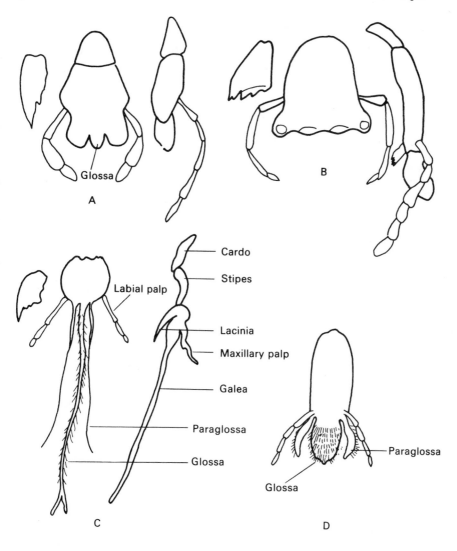

Figure 4.33 *Mouthparts of some Hymenoptera* A sawfly B short tongued wasp C long tongued wasp D short tongued bee (mandibles and maxillae not shown) This figure in conjunction with Figure 4.34 shows how the lengthening of the glossae has occurred in both wasps and bees.

boscis and it becomes flaccid, but the coiling is caused by contraction of its intrinsic muscles. When they suck most Lepidoptera rest with their feet on the flower, but some of the long-tongued moths hover. That is especially true of those which suck nectar from the base of long corolla-tubes. The proboscis of such a moth may be over twelve centimetres long (much longer than its body) and the problem of drawing nectar whilst hovering resembles that of aircraft refuelling in the air. Even in the shorter-tongued individuals the coiling of the proboscis presents a mechanical problem. In order to provide sufficient flexibility in the proboscis, as well as to give enough support to a long fluid-laden tube, the cuticle of the galeae is thick but divided up into rings rather in the manner of a mammalian trachea.

The Lepidoptera have adapted to nectar sucking by the extreme development of one part of the mouthparts. The nectar-sucking Hymenoptera, too, are economical in the parts which make up their proboscis, but have used the glossa of the labium instead of the galeae. Whereas virtually all Lepidoptera are nectar-sucking most adult Hymenoptera have biting mouthparts. They all have the two glossae fused into one structure which, in the more primitive nectar-feeders, is short and, being covered in hairs, serves as an effective licking organ. In the more advanced forms the glossa is elongated and becomes a sucking proboscis. Figure 4.33 shows some of the modifications: they do not necessarily represent an evolutionary sequence.

Figure 4.34 shows the ultimate stage, in the hive bee. The maxilla has lost most of the lacinia and palp, leaving the much enlarged galea. The labium has greatly reduced paraglossae but the glossa is long and so are the palps. When the bee sucks the flabellum (end part of the glossa) is dipped into the nectar which is drawn up, almost flung up, by a succession of shortenings and extensions of the glossa. When the nectar has been raised to a sufficient height its subsequent transport is taken over by the pumping action of the pharynx. The elongated labial palps and galeae act as guards to protect the glossa when it is at rest, and when in use they lie alongside it and contribute to the sucking-tube without apparently being essential to it because the glossa can suck from corolla-tubes which are much longer than the galeae. So again we find that the sucking action depends essentially on just one structure. The mandibles which, in the Lepidoptera, were wholly reduced remain functional in the Hymenoptera but play no part in sucking.

In some Diptera 'mandibles' do form part of the piercing and sucking apparatus. Dipteran mandibles are never of the biting type. They occur as stylets in the females of some blood-sucking forms (Figure 4.35): there is doubt as to whether they are homologues of the mandibles in other insects but in view of their position it is convenient to use the term. The main piercing organs are the barbed laciniae of the maxillae: the mandibles are said to play a minor role. The hypopharynx has to be as elongated as the stylets in order to bring the anticoagulant to the wound. The labrum-epipharynx which is concave on its posterior (lower) surface has, by lying in the deeply grooved labium, the function of forming a food canal.

The Diptera have undergone great evolutionary changes so that in the most advanced Sub-Order, the Cyclorrhapha, the mouthparts bear little obvious resemblance to preceding forms. The typical cyclorrhaphan condition is exemplified by the house-fly (Figure 4.36). The structure is very complicated and the diagrams do

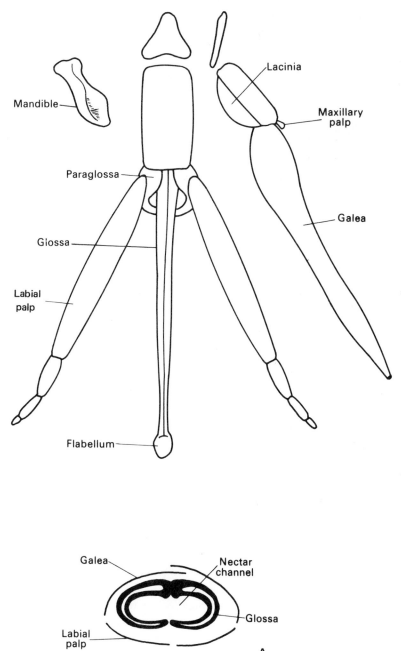

Figure 4.34 *Mouthparts of a hive bee* A Section across the proboscis

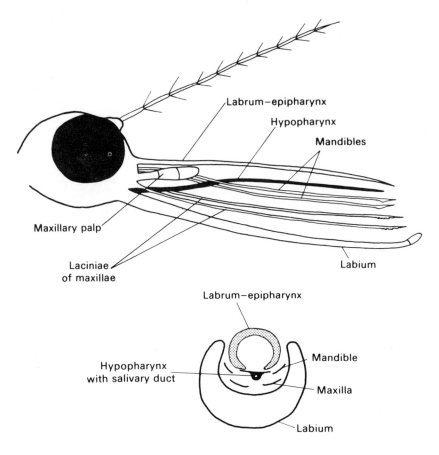

Figure 4.35 *Head and mouthparts of a mosquito*

no more than show the general plan. Mandibles are missing and so are maxillae, except for reduced palps. The labium (curved upwards) forms the base of the proboscis and the labrum (curved downwards) its lid: their relationship is similar to the condition in the mosquito (see the sectional drawing in Figure 4.35). The hypopharynx (pierced by the salivary duct) lies between the labium and labrum — again as in the mosquito. The rest of the proboscis bears no resemblance to other Diptera. The tip of the labium is composed of two labella — sucking pads — on the surface of which open a number of fine tubes — the pseudotracheae — which at their proximal ends join to form a short duct which receives the secretion of the salivary gland. The furca is a supporting structure in each labellum. The remaining structures are concerned with exerting a pumping action in the proboscis. By a complicated process which involves extension of air sacs, muscle contraction and blood pressure the entire proboscis can be stiffened and brought down to the position shown in Figure 4.36A. The fulcrum, an internal extension of the head casing, serves as a base for some of the muscles and the apodemes serve for articulation of the labrum. The labella, when they are turgid, are pressed on to the sub-

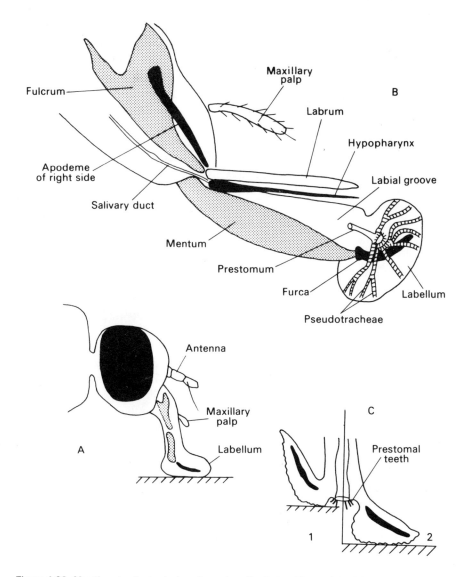

Figure 4.36 *Mouthparts of a typical cyclorraphan fly* **A** head from right side with proboscis extended **B** details of the mouthparts **C** front view of proboscis in two operating positions: **1** direct feeding position **2** filtering position

stance which is about to be eaten as in Figure 4.36C2, and the food (after preliminary breakdown by salivary enzymes) is sucked up in liquid form through the pseudotracheae and along a channel between the labrum and hypopharynx into the alimentary canal. In position C1 the labella are lifted off the surface so that the opening of the prestomum is applied directly to the food. In this position not only liquids but particles can be sucked up. Furthermore by the action of the prestomal teeth a certain amount of scraping of the surface is possible.

The mechanism is a sophisticated adaptation to sucking either existing liquids or solids which are first rendered liquid by enzyme action, as in the blow fly. The Diptera have made great use of the proboscis in exploiting a wide variety of ecological niches ranging from sucking the exposed nectar of flowers, the juices of rotting fruit, or fungi and organic debris generally. In addition, by their process of external digestion, they can act as primary agents of corpse decomposition. Some have also become blood-suckers, as we shall see.

The hover-flies (Syrphidae) are a large group all of whose members are nectar-feeders: they have the typical cyclorrhaphan proboscis. They hover over flowers whose nectar is easily accessible, moving rapidly from flower to flower and, having settled, feed rapidly before moving on. They have to confine their activity to times when nectar is flowing because they feed on nothing else and are therefore usually to be seen in the sun. This wholly carbohydrate diet in the adult stage is possible because the larvae are highly successful protein feeders, their prey including large numbers of aphids. It seems strange that such a successful group should not have adapted its proboscis for taking concealed nectar from long corolla-tubes. Some hover-flies have slightly lengthened the rostrum and labella, widening their range of suitable flowers, but the Family seems to be an example of great success in a particular adaptation which has not called for further modification. The large number of umbelliferous flowers and other 'open' types satisfies their demands.

The cyclorrhaphan blood-suckers, of which the tsetse is by far the most important, have what seems a rough and ready way of penetrating the skin. Being cyclorrhaphan they have lost both mandibles and maxillae: there are no stylets. The proboscis consists (Figure 4.37) of the firm labium within which lie the labrum and hypopharynx. The sides of the labium enclose these two structures totally and

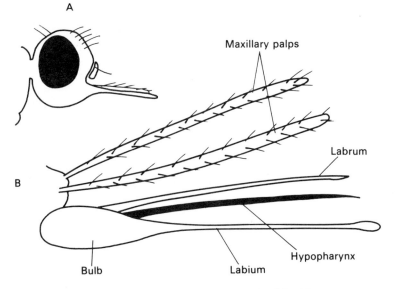

Figure 4.37 *Head and mouthparts of tsetse-fly* **A** head from the right side **B** proboscis

there are many locking devices to ensure that in the jabbing position the three components of the proboscis act as one unit. The proboscis is turned down and simply thrust into the skin of the host.

The piercing and sucking habit was first established in the Hemiptera, and the group is very uniform in the method which it employs today. Most of our detailed knowledge of the feeding mechanism is about aphids which have been studied closely on account of their economic importance. The mechanical problem which faces an aphid when it begins to feed is great. Whereas a blood-sucker has to penetrate only a short distance beneath the epidermis in order to reach a capillary, the phloem is more deeply situated. In addition there is a great penetration problem. Once the mammal's horny layer has been pierced the rest of the penetration is easy because only cells and cell membranes stand in the way of the stylets. Plant cell walls, however, offer far more resistance. Consequently bugs thrust their stylets between rather than through the epidermal and cortical cells. Not until the phloem has been reached do the stylets penetrate into the cells. This process calls for the secretion of an enzyme in the saliva to break down the intercellular bonding. Clearly the stylets will have to steer a circuitous course through the tissues, so that control will tend to be lost and the insect may not be able to exert enough pressure at the end to push the stylets into the phloem cells. Two adaptations cater for this contingency. A further secretion of the salivary glands produces a protein stylet sheath which probably helps to bind the long stylets together as they descend (it is rather like the cement lining which is applied to the sides and roof of a tunnel as it is bored), and in addition the points of the mandibular stylets, which perform the main work of penetrating, are very sharp.[1] Figure 4.38 shows the mouthparts of a plant bug.

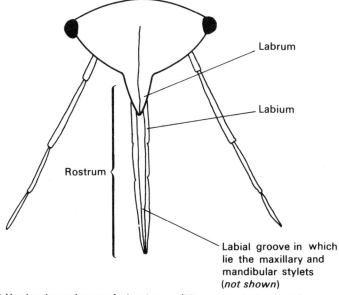

Labrum

Labium

Rostrum

Labial groove in which lie the maxillary and mandibular stylets (*not shown*)

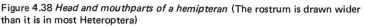

Figure 4.38 *Head and mouthparts of a hemipteran* (The rostrum is drawn wider than it is in most Heteroptera)

All Homoptera are phytophagous (plant-feeders), but the Heteroptera include many members which suck the blood of insects and vertebrates. The predacious forms have shorter rostra than do the phytophagous ones, for the reason already explained (see the reduviid in Figure 2.9). The Heteroptera also include the lesser water boatmen (Corixidae) which have lost the ability to penetrate living tissues and instead feed on debris at the bottom of ponds, sucking it up by means of a short proboscis, rather like a vacuum cleaner.

Parasitism

It is not remarkable that so numerous a group as the insects should include some parasitic members. Adaptive radiation is demonstrated by the number of times that the parasitic habit has arisen in different Orders. We have seen an instance of it in the Coleoptera. Some Orders are wholly ectoparasitic, eg the Siphunculata (sucking lice) and Siphonaptera (fleas). In several Orders various ectoparasitic habits have evolved independently, eg the Diptera (mosquitoes), the Heteroptera (blood sucking bugs) and the special case of the Hymenoptera (ichneumons), whilst the Strepsiptera (stylopids) have evolved the most extreme adaptation of all and are endoparasitic.

The fleas and sucking lice are profoundly modified, having become secondarily wingless (Figure 2.15 and 4.39) The adult fleas's extremely laterally flattened body enables it to move through the thick fur of mammals. The long outward bent claws and the stiff spines on the legs and body give it a good grip on the fur. Compound eyes are lacking, though some species have reduced simple eyes, and the antennae are vestigial. The mouthparts are adapted for piercing and sucking. The most modified parts are the hind-legs which are very long, the coxae being long and broad and the femora broad: even the tibiae are broad, whereas in most insects they are narrow. The non-parasitic larva is mobile, while the pupae of some species bear wing cases which suggests that the wingless condition has been fairly recently evolved. Even within such a small and specialized group as the fleas adaptive radiation has occurred. Most are parasitic on placental mammals, with some species on marsupials, others on birds, and one even on a snake, so that physiological adaptation to feeding on poikilotherms has evolved.

Behaviour too has evolved. The eggs are laid on the ground and the larvae live in dirt, forming a silken cocoon in which they pupate. All parasites have the problem of finding a host and the fleas have solved it by a unique adaptation. After pupation the adult does not immediately emerge from the cocoon but can remain inactive for a long time, without needing to feed. The vibrations set up by a passing mammal or bird provide the stimulus for activity to begin and, since jumps of over fifty milli-metres in height are normal, the adults are able to land on some part of the host, after which they rely on their other adaptations for moving through the hair. Fleas which parasitize large mammals such as deer have greater powers of vertical jumping than do those which live on rats, whilst the mole flea cannot jump at all.

The most interesting adaptation is the way in which the fleas, on becoming apterous, have used features of their former wing mechanism for jumping. As we

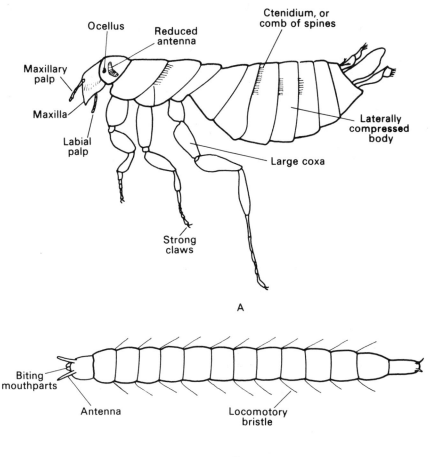

Figure 4.39 *Adult and larval flea* **A** adult mole flea **B** a flea larva

saw in Chapter 1 flight is not merely a matter of antagonistic muscles pulling on the wings but the result of a complex system in the thorax whose intrinsic elasticity plays an important part. The elasticity is brought about partly by the way in which thoracic plates are arranged in relation to each other but also by the presence of the elastic rubber-like protein, resilin, at the wing-hinge ligament of some insects in which direct flight muscles are important. As a propellant resilin has two advantages over muscle which are of great value to the fleas: first its action is independent of temperature and, secondly, it can yield its maximum effect immediately whereas muscle needs time to build up maximum contraction. A resilin-based system therefore enables a 'cold' flea to jump on to a new host from the ground by making a very big, sudden, jump.

The following brief account of the jumping mechanism is based on a hypothesis recently proposed.[2] When a flea is preparing to jump it raises the femora and brings the trochanters into contact with the substratum. It then has to load the force of muscular contraction into the patch of resilin in the thoracic wall. That is accomplished by the contraction of former flight muscles which distort the thoracic box and squeeze the resilin patch.

The thorax is shortened by contraction of longitudinal muscles. The internal ridges which stiffen the cuticle are thereby aligned into continuous lines of force along which the thrust of the straightening leg will be directed. The thoracic segments are held in their new position by cuticular catches (pegs and sockets on the exoskeleton), and the flea is then in the cocked state, ready to jump.

The jump is initiated by relaxation of the muscles which raised the femora and shortened the thorax. Consequently the femora descend (Figure 4.40) and thrust the tibiae hard against the substratum whilst the release of the catches allows the natural shape of the thorax to reassert itself, thrusting down along the lines of force into the trochanters. In addition the energy stored in the resilin amplifies the acceleration.

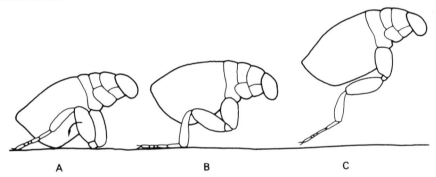

A   B   C

Figure 4.40 *Stages in the leap of the flea* A pre-jumping position with femora raised and about to be swung down in direction of arrow B downward rotation of the femora has forced the tibiae against the substratum C take-off

The other important parasitic Order is that of sucking lice, the Siphunculata. They are all parasitic on mammals, being transferred from one individual to another through contact: there is no free-living stage. Consequently many features of the body are reduced (Figure 4.41): the antennae are short, eyes are never important and are absent in some species, the body shows lack of segmentation and wings are missing. The principal adaptations to ectoparasitic life are the dorso-ventral flattening of the body, the very powerful gripping legs for holding on to mammalian hair and the highly specialized mouthparts which do not closely resemble those of other Orders. There are three stylets derived from the hypopharynx and labium. Prior to their penetration of the skin the louse anchors itself to the host by means of the small teeth on the haustellum. The pharyngeal tube is then thrust into the wound and, acting as a hose, allows blood to be pumped from the host by muscular action of the pharyngeal muscles.

The biting lice (Mallophaga, Figure 4.41) resemble the Siphunculata in their general ectoparasitic adaptations: aptery, reduced sense organs and flattened shape, but not in their mouthparts. They have strong biting mouthparts, although most

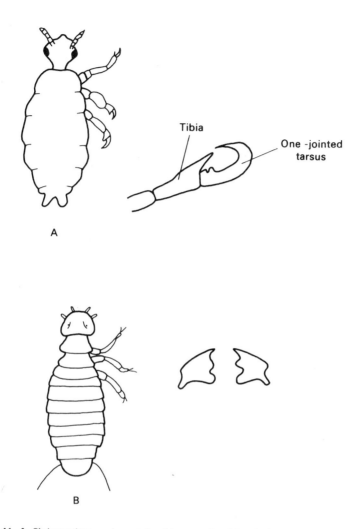

Figure 4.41 **A** Siphunculata : a human head louse and a claw of a hog-louse **B** Mallophaga : a mallophagan together with diagram of strong biting mandibles

components apart from the mandibles are reduced. They feed on the hair and feathers of living mammals and birds.

The most extreme adaptation to parasitic life is found in a small Order, the Strepsiptera. The larva enters the larval body of the host, usually a bee, wasp or plant bug, and develops there while the host pupates. Towards the end of its larval life the strepsipteran larva thrusts its head through the side of the host pupa by piercing an intersegmental membrane. Subsequent development depends on the sex of the parasite. If it is a male it pupates and eventually emerges as an adult which, in spite of many atypical features behaves as a free-living flying insect (Figure 4.42). The female, however, after pupation keeps her position in the host, which she never leaves. Her adult body retains larval features. She absorbs food from the host

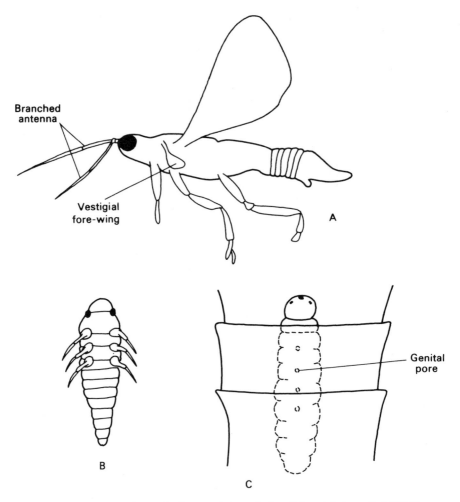

Figure 4.42 *Strepsiptera* **A** a male **B** ventral view of a free-living early larva **C** a female with head and thorax projecting between segments of host's body

through her cuticle and all her external features are reduced. She is virtually a static reproductive organ. The male fertilizes her *in situ* and she gives rise viviparously to larvae which escape from the host. Since the hosts tend to congregate on flowers, the emerging larvae find no difficulty in climbing on to an adult member of the host species. If it is a bee or wasp it carries the strepsipteran larva to its nest where the parasite enters one of the host larvae. The parasite has peculiar effects on its host, including alteration of specific characters, sex reversal and even castration.

On morphological grounds the Strepsiptera are thought to be related to the Coleoptera (we saw an instance of larval parasitism in the Meloïdae), and a very few of them are not parasitic at all. It seems strange that only one Order of insects should have evolved adult parasitism, for the adaptation does result in good dispersal and biological economy.

Aquatic adaptations

Before leaving the subject of adaptive radiation it is worth looking at the way in which some insects other than the Coleoptera have succeeded in making use of water as an environment. Examples can be found in most Orders, so we shall confine ourselves to a few which present particularly interesting adaptive features.

The Hemiptera have made great use of fresh water. Some like the Notonectidae and Corixidae are fast swimmers but others are adapted to living on the surface. The water surface might not seem a prepossessing environment but it does provide plenty of food in the form of live and dead insects, for many small ones are blown there and, having alighted, are unable to take off again. The reader will have observed the struggles of small insects which have fallen on to water. Not only can they not fly away, they can scarcely move forward at all, even on the surface. The surface-living insect has to overcome the problem of support and locomotion on the surface skin of the water. The pond-skaters (Veliidae and Gerridae, Figure 2.9) overcome the danger of adhesion to the water film by having a thick ventral covering of unwettable hairs so that the body is not actually in contact with the water. That is an added precaution lest they should touch the water, for in practice their ventral surface is normally held clear of it by the legs; perhaps when the water surface is disturbed by the wind there is a danger of the underside being wetted. The tarsal claws are ante-apical, that is to say they are set well back from the tip of the last segment which ends instead in a tuft of hairs. This device gives a large blunt tip to the foot and prevents it sinking into the water. The camel's splayed foot is analogous.

The pond-skaters dart rapidly across the surface. Their fore-legs are short and, although not morphologically adapted, are used for holding the prey. Locomotion is carried out by the very long middle-legs assisted by the hind-legs. The action is similar to rowing except that the tarsi do not actually break the surface film. The middle-legs beat in unison: they press into the film on the power stroke and on the recovery stroke the tarsae are lifted clear of the surface so that the insects can almost be said to hop along the surface.

The water measurers (Hydrometridae) are close relatives of the pond-skaters. Their locomotion is very slow, and their six limbs are moved in the usual sequence (page 76). The same applies to some pond-skaters when they move slowly. *Hydrometra* (Figure 4.43) has a highly elongated body as well as long legs which are presumably advantageous because they lead to a greater moment at their tip than would short ones and are therefore able to overcome surface tension.

Concluding remarks

We have seen something of the extent to which the insect body plan is capable of meeting the challenge of different ways of life. Adaptive radiation is what evolution is about. It is not enough, however, for organisms to adapt their structure. Each environment and each way of life within an environment, calls for total adaptation of physiology and behaviour as well as of structure: we shall examine some aspects

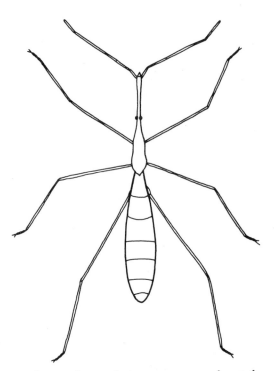

Figure 4.43 *A water measurer*

of these adaptations in the next chapter. In conclusion we may wonder at the insects' failure to adapt to marine life. Very few are at home in salt water. Some apterygotes, earwigs and beetles which frequent the sea shore live in the saline environment of the spray zone and may even enter the water; a few mosquitoes breed in brackish water. It is not immediately obvious why insects should shun the sea, especially in view of the readiness with which they have taken to fresh water and the fact that many of their terrestrial adaptations would seem to be quite useful in water. The answer probably lies in physiology and ecology. The land provides so many habitats in which insects have become thoroughly and pre-eminently established that the necessary pressure to exploit a totally new environment, with its great challenge of osmotic and salt balance difficulties, may not have arisen. All the ecological niches that insects might be expected to occupy in the sea are probably already better filled by the large number of crustaceans that have radiated into them.

References

1 DIXON,A.F.G. (1973). *Biology of aphids.* London: Edward Arnold.
2 ROTHSCHILD,M., SCHLEIN,Y., PARKER,K., NEVILLE,A.C. &
    STERNBERG,S. The flying leap of the flea. *Scientific American*
    March 1973.
For detailed information on locomotion in terrestrial insects:
HUGHES,G.M. Locomotion: terrestrial. In *The physiology of Insecta,*
    Ed. M. Rockstein (1955). vol.2. New York: Academic Press.

Part II
The Supremacy of the Insects

Chapter 5
Behaviour and Ecology

This could easily be the longest chapter. It is almost impossible to consider behaviour and ecology separately for each concerns what the animal *does*. A study of behaviour could include the minute examination of sense organs and nerve mechanism, but in this book we are as far as possible taking a broad look at the insect condition rather than studying minutiae for their own sake. We shall consider behaviour in relation to the insects' response to their environment, in particular the relationship of insects with plants, their social life and their use of protective mechanisms.

It is usual to describe insect behaviour as instinctive, that is to say that their responses to the challenge of the environment are inborn, learned neither from their parents nor from other members of their species nor acquired by experience, and therefore predictable in any set of circumstances. It follows that the individual insect cannot adapt its behaviour to suit environmental conditions for which it is 'programmed'. Adaptation can take place in the species by the normal selective action of the environment which plays on variability amongst members of a population, but the individual insect cannot adapt itself to new conditions: it cannot learn. Insect behaviour, however, is not as straightforward as that. It all depends on what is meant by learning. There does seem to be a dearth of evidence for the individual insect being able to make use of previously gained experience in order to cope with a completely new environmental challenge. (It may even be argued that the term *experience* should be confined to information which the organism retains to some extent, instead of being used indiscriminately to mean all that has happened to it: it is difficult to avoid loose terminology in this field.) Instances of adaptation to feeding on materials which they would not normally encounter in nature do not imply learning to cope: they apply to insects with generalized feeding habits incidentally tackling a new substance as part of their normal behaviour.

In the vast majority of insects learned behaviour, even if it exists, cannot be passed on to subsequent generations through imitation of parental behaviour by the offspring because in very few species do the offspring meet their parents. (There is no reason to believe that insects inherit characteristics which their parents have acquired more than do any other animals.) Although learning can occur, stereotyped patterns certainly constitute the greater part of the insects' behaviour. Again, we must ask what we mean by stereotyped behaviour. It does

not mean that the response must be identical in every respect, but that it follows
the same pattern. For instance, grasshoppers make a chirping sound (stridulation) by
scraping a row of pegs on the inner surface of the hind femur against a vein on
the fore-wing of the same side. Different species have characteristic songs, which
serve to bring the sexes together for mating and probably also keep members of the
species in proximity to each other as a valuable prelude to actual mating. The song
of a particular species is of a fixed pattern, but its intensity depends on the stimulus
which the individual receives. So stereotyped is the song that if grasshopper nymphs
are reared from the egg in the laboratory their song, as adults, is wholly characteristic of their species. Not even exposure to the song of other species will affect
the result.

The complex process whereby a female ichneumon selects the host caterpillar
and paralyses it is the result of inborn patterns. The same applies to the even more
complex behaviour of the solitary wasps which, at a distance of several metres from
their nest, sting and paralyse spiders and, having pulled them to the nest, lay eggs
in them. There are several Families of wasps which provision their nests with caterpillars or other insects, and in each case the *right* sequence of events follows from
the release of an innate pattern of behaviour. Not only these sophisticated patterns
but the whole life of insects is really a catalogue of pre-set reflexes and it does not
seem that the ability to learn plays a role of any importance in their lives. That behaviour patterns are genetically fixed is supported by experimental evidence.
Species of the same genus are chosen for the purpose, each species having some
peculiarity of behaviour which marks it off from its close relative. The Orthoptera
which form inter-specific hybrids fairly readily are particularly suitable. It has been
shown that several features of behaviour are inherited Mendelially — for instance
some characteristics of song are passed on as if they are under the control of dominant genes in one species and of recessive genes in the other while other characteristics reveal the action of incomplete dominance between the alleles of the parent
species. The evidence allows for no doubt that genetic control of behaviour patterns
is widespread.

The fact that learning is not an important aspect of most insect behaviour
patterns does not mean that insects lack the *ability* to learn. Even primitive insects
can be made to respond to 'reward and punishment' tests, which is not surprising
since associative learning is possible at much lower evolutionary levels too — in
Nereis for example. If the insect's normal behaviour leads, in the experiment, to
unpleasant consequences (such as electric shocks) it can reverse its normal behaviour. If a bee is presented with a sugar solution it extends its proboscis in order
to suck. If it is offered an odorous solution at the same time as the sugar solution,
and then after a certain number of presentations the sugar is removed the bee
will continue to extend its proboscis in response to the odorous solution. This
training is reminiscent of the original Pavlovian experiment with dog, food and
bell, but does not ask quite as much of the bee as was asked of the dog because,
whereas there was no natural relationship between food and bell, odour is very
often associated with nectar in nature. Whilst this kind of learning certainly suggests
a basis on which new patterns of behaviour can be built it is not to be thought of

as intelligent behaviour at all — indeed if anything the reverse, for one could claim that the bee, like Pavlov's dog, has been taught to make a mistake!

Another form of learning is to be seen in phytophagous (plant-eating) insects which change their habits according to the plant on which the larvae are reared. If the sub-species of the ermine moth *Hyponomeuta padella,* whose caterpillars feed on apple leaves and whose adults lay their eggs on apple, is presented in captivity with hawthorn instead it will adapt to the alternative plant. It will not prosper there, some of the adults so produced being infertile, but up to a point it can be said to have learned the feeding habits of the sub-species which is normally associated with hawthorn. The willow sawfly, *Pontania salicis,* if forced to oviposit on a species of willow which is not natural to it, will accept the alternative rather than not lay its eggs at all. For the first few generations larval mortality is high but it decreases in successive generations until a stage is reached at which the emerging adults not only accept the 'wrong' willow species but actually select it if they are given the opportunity of choosing between it and the original species. They have become conditioned during larval life. In these last two examples the larva's learning process seems to resemble the imprinting learning of vertebrates, especially birds, in which the young animal accepts the features of the first active objects which it sees as those of its own species, normally its own parents in the act of bringing it food.

The most striking examples of learning come, of course, from the social Hymenoptera. Von Frisch's work on the way in which foraging bees learn the route to their flower crop and impart the information to the members of the hive who, in turn, learn the distance and direction from them, is well known. He was able to show that bees discriminate colours, shapes, tastes and odours and associate them with food. Since the ability to associate is lost after a while if the food ceases to be linked with the associated condition it is fair to describe the retention of the information as memory.

The bee's brain is certainly involved in the ability to associate colour with food, but some learning can occur at a lower level of an organism's nervous organization. Decapitation experiments have shown that, in the locust and cockroach, leg movements can be learned through the medium of thoracic ganglia. The headless insect can be placed in such a position that lowering its leg causes it to receive an electric shock. After many shocks the leg is lowered less frequently. This could be interpreted as a simple physiological mechanism, not necessarily associated with learning but Horridge[1] was able to show that an untrained headless control animal, when placed in the same experimental situation as the trained one, allowed itself to receive more shocks than did the trained one because it kept its leg raised for shorter periods of time. This kind of experiment sheds light on the manner in which the movements of different limbs of a complex animal may be controlled — for example all three pairs of an insect's legs may not perform similar tasks. We have seen how in carnivorous aquatic beetles the fore-legs are locomotory, in jumping orthopterans the hind-legs alone are involved in jumping — and so on. There is presumably an advantage in having certain routine movements under localized control.

The observations on localized 'learning' do not alter the fact that individual insects possess extremely restricted powers of learning. They are limited as to what they are able to learn, and in a general sense it is fair to say that an individual's reaction to a given situation is predictable.

We shall now consider some instances of the flexibility in the Class as a whole which has arisen from the insects' stereotyped behaviour.

The relationship between insects and plants

On account of the great economic importance of phytophagous insects, and because insects are so commonly found on plants, we generally think of the higher plants as providing the major source of food for insects. That view is only partly true. If we consider the insects as a whole we find that phytophagy is a major form of feeding in only about a third of the Orders.[2a] On the other hand carnivores and scavengers are to be found in respectively, half and more than half of the Orders.

It seems that the leaves of higher plants are unable to provide enough protein and fat for most insects. Carnivores are likely to find the most necessary food substances, and certainly the proteins and fats, in their prey but are faced with the problem of catching it. Scavengers have many advantages, for not only is their food material readily available in large quantities but it contains microorganisms whose synthesis of essential substances makes up for what the living plant tissues lack. Scavenging and microbial feeding, closely followed by the carnivorous habit, are primitive, whilst feeding on the leaves of higher plants is a much later development. The really successful phytophagous insects have solved the problem of using plant substances, especially fats, which could not satisfy other insects, but even so they exist on a nutritional knife edge for their success in any particular year or any particular place depends on the state of the crop which they exploit. Nitrogen deficiency, for example, in the soil has been shown to impede development and fecundity in several groups of insects through its effect on the plant crop. It is not a case of the plants failing to grow, but failing to produce sufficient protein to meet the insects needs.

Another factor which accounts for the relative paucity of phytophagous insect Orders is the physical difficulty of staying on the plant. The waxy nature of plant cuticle was evolved as a defence against water loss, but it also makes it difficult for insects to grip the leaves. Many insects, including larvae, find it easier to confine themselves to the edge of a leaf, or to a large vein, using the legs on each side for gripping the surfaces. The larvae of Lepidoptera and some Hymenoptera, which are the most successful foliage feeders, have evolved pro-legs whose large area give a better grip than could be obtained by the thoracic legs alone. In addition the pro-legs of the Lepidoptera are equipped with a group of chitinous hooks, the crotchets, which further enhance the grip. Many phytophagous larvae, particularly those of the Diptera, avoid the problem by living not on the surface of leaves but inside them as leaf-miners. Their activity can be detected by the burrows they make in the tissues of the leaf blade, often just under the epidermis so that pale streaks can be seen when the leaf is held up to the light.

Some plants can discourage insects from attacking them by means of their thick cuticle (one rarely sees a holly leaf which has been nibbled) or by means of a dense covering of hairs which makes walking on them difficult. Others have evolved a more subtle method, biochemical protection.[2b] They produce sterols that closely resemble the hormone ecdysone, secreted by the insects' prothoracic gland, which controls ecdysis: insect larvae which feed on these plants undergo premature ecdysis. This has been demonstrated experimentally by injecting locust hoppers with the plant hormone gibberellin. It is thought that the gibberellin stimulates neurosecretory cells near the brain to secrete hormones which then stimulate the prothoracic gland, but the gibberellin's action in the insect body is not fully understood.

Insects may be polyphagous (feeding on several species of plants) or mono-phagous. In either case the first stage in feeding is the selection of a suitable plant which, especially in monophagous insects, calls for a high degree of discrim-ination. (The term *plant predator* is sometimes used to describe animals which feed on living plant tissues as opposed to those which scavenge on dead plants.)

Amongst the most successful plant feeders are the larvae of Lepidoptera, an Order which is almost exclusively phytophagous in both the larval and adult stages. Many lepidopteran larvae are monophagous or confine themselves to a group of related plant species: few are general feeders. How then, does a caterpillar select the right plant? Usually the selection is made by the ovipositing female and not primarily by the caterpillar, but females not infrequently oviposit on an unsuit-able plant or on an unsuitable part of the right host plant. It has been shown, for example, the caterpillars of the gipsy moth *Lymantria dispar* select mature alder leaves as against young ones if they are offered a choice. Again, starvation will induce the larvae of the ermine moth which feeds, say, on apple to feed on leaves of the 'wrong' tree, but when they are offered a choice they select those on which their parents were reared. Physical factors such as rain or wind may shake eggs off the plant on which they were laid, and in some Families the eggs are not placed in position by the female but simply dropped from her in flight.

It is, therefore, important that caterpillars should be able to recognize the right plant. The visual sense is only marginally important as a means of recog-nition; the principal one is chemical, and is remarkable for the extremely simple morphology of the receptor organs[2c] which consist of only a small number of cells. The main receptor sites are olfactory ones on the antennae, and olfactory and gustatory ones on the maxillary palps; removal of both these organs destroys much of the caterpillars' ability to discriminate between plants which are nor-mally acceptable and those which are not. If, in addition, the epipharynx and hypopharynx are removed discrimination is completely lost.

The principal taste receptors are on the maxillary sensilla styloconica which lie very close to the mouth. Most caterpillars appear to possess sugar and salt receptors, a state of affairs which is probably common amongst terrestrial arthropods. By means of their antennae some woodlice can distinguish between water and dilute solutions of sucrose or of salt, and some centipedes can certainly discriminate between water and sucrose. Caterpillars, however, push discrimination much further, species being sensitive in varying degrees to the taste of substances associated with particular groups of plants.

Communication and social behaviour

Most animals can be said to have some degree of social organization, if only for the purpose of sexual reproduction which entails the need to locate at least the approximate position of the opposite sex and, in animals which have internal fertilization, to unite with a partner. In most insects social organization does not extend beyond that level but, because of their small size and their considerable dispersal owing to the power of flight, they often employ sophisticated means of signalling and of species recognition. The essential feature of social organization is communication. Only a very few insects have pushed social organization to the level of living in established communities: the phenomenon is confined to the advanced Hymenoptera and the termites (Isoptera). The more sophisticated the level of social organization the more elaborate must be the means of communication, as when the tasks performed by the various members of a colony have to be co-ordinated according to the collective needs of the community.

Communication at lower levels is not confined to the needs of sexual reproduction — indeed it is useful to communicate with predators by giving them either misleading information or due warning. It is perhaps stretching a point to describe *concealment* as communication — but it is a kind of positive non-communication because concealment means making a predator mistake potential prey for some inedible object.

Protection against predators

Many insects are almost staple foods of animals such as birds, reptiles and amphibians as well as of other insects. They protect themselves by a variety of behavioural devices as well as by specially adapted external features. We are not concerned with making a catalogue of all the ways but rather with bringing out the connections between the various defensive mechanisms (devices) and the insects' ecology. Defence against predators implies defence at each stage of the life history, but we shall concentrate on the active exposed stages — chiefly the adult but also the larvae of many species and of course the nymphs of Exopterygota generally. Perhaps the most vulnerable stages of all are the larvae of phytophagous forms which feed on the outside of plants, and adults which feed openly and have to fly in exposed places in order to find mates. Many insects mate early in their adult lives: their protection has, therefore, to be effective but not necessarily of long duration. That is why towards the end of the season one sees many butterflies with damaged wings fluttering weakly and being easily picked off by birds: their protection has lasted long enough for eggs to be laid.

Concealment

Concealment is usually a matter of the insect resembling the colour of its background, or appearing to form a part of the object on which it is resting. Protection of the eggs is fairly easily solved by their small size and oviposition in concealed places. Eggs which will give rise to herbivorous larvae, however, have to be laid on or near the prospective food material — or else *in* it, which solves the problem of concealment completely. Butterflies' eggs, which are usually laid on plants, are almost always cryptically (i.e. protectively) coloured.

Crypsis in insects is usually a property of those which serve as prey rather than of the predators. That is different from what happens in birds and mammals; for example the colour of the lion and the markings of the cat family serve to conceal them from their prey which is also, though differently, cryptically coloured. Presumably the greater visual acuity of vertebrates accounts for this, and also the fact that flying predators cannot be concealed.

We do not propose to give a descriptive catalogue of the various examples of crypsis, which are better seen in books of coloured illustrations. They are of course seen best of all in nature, but since by definition they are not easily observed it helps to know what one is looking for.

The later larvae and the pupae, which are large enough to attract attention but lack the ability to escape, are vulnerable and so, for different reasons, are the adults.

A type of crypsis which has been extensively studied and which demonstrates its selective advantage is the appearance in smoke-polluted industrial areas of melanic forms of species that elsewhere are not black. Many moths display this phenomenon, the best documented one being the peppered moth, *Biston betularia,* which until the middle nineteenth century, was known only in the pale *betularia* form. The wings are peppered with small black marks on white, which produces excellent concealment when the moths rest in daytime with wings extended on lichen-covered tree trunks. In industrial regions where tree trunks were blackened with soot the melanic form, *carbonaria,* became much more common than the typical one: the first *carbonaria* was recorded in Manchester in 1847 and by 1895 ninety eight per cent of the population there, was black. Kettlewell has demonstrated that the melanic forms have a clear advantage in smoke-blackened areas and the *betularia* form in rural areas because the principal predators are birds, which, hunting by sight, pick the resting moths off the trees. He released known numbers of moths, marked on the underside of the wing, into a wood near Birmingham and one in Dorset. The chief predators were the robin *Erithacus rubecula,* hedge sparrow *Prunella modularis* and spotted flycatcher *Muscicapa striata.* When he subsequently trapped moths in the same woods using a mercury vapour lamp at night he found that a far higher proportion of melanics than of *betularia* was recaptured from the Birmingham wood, but the reverse was true in Dorset. Since predation by night-flying birds and by bats must be at a much lower level and is probably indiscriminate it follows that the light and dark forms each constitute crypsis on appropriate backgrounds against predation by diurnal birds. The *carbonaria* form depends on the action of a single gene acting as a dominant, which accounts for the short time that melanic forms took to become preponderant in industrial areas. Now, two important facts have emerged. First, the figure of ninety eight per cent melanics in the worst-polluted areas has not risen to one hundred per cent and, secondly, melanic forms have spread (though not in such high proportions) into rural areas that are apparently unaffected by smoke pollution and where, on grounds of protective colouration alone, the melanic condition should be disadvantageous. These observations show how unwise it is to consider any biological phenomenon in isolation. The *carbonaria* gene extends into rural areas through the operation of hybrid vigour. There is no reason to suppose that the *carbonaria* locus affects colour alone, and its presence even in the heterozygote may have benefi-cial effects apart from those of adult crypsis. Pollution may occur, even in the absence of manifestly obvious deposition of soot, by toxic substances being blown from the industrial region into the countryside, as had happened in Eng-land when prevailing winds have caused pollution to the east of industrial towns. Leaf-eating larvae are particularly vulnerable to poisoning by pollution, and it is thought that the *carbonaria* allele confers a physiological advantage in that situation even though the larvae are not melanic. The heterozygotes are more likely to sur-vive than are the homozygotes because any lethal mutations which arise at loci close to the advantageous allele will be sheltered in the dominant condition of the advantageous allele, because proximity will minimize their chances of being separated from it at crossing-over, and will produce a high mortality rate of the homozygotes. In the heterozygotes, on the other hand, their effect will be less damaging. Consequently a population comes to contain a larger proportion of heterozygotes than would be predicted mathematically, which encourages the survival of a sizeable number of the recessive genes. The *betularia* phenotype therefore continues to appear in a regular, though small, proportion in heavily-polluted areas in spite of its selective disadvantage.

This is a suitable point at which to draw attention to the danger of confusing apparently similar phenomena. Industrial melanism exists also in the two-spot ladybird, *Adalia bipunctata*, whose typical form has one black spot in the centre of each red wing cover. The gene which determines it, is recessive to two alleles that produce black elytra each with either two or three red spots. In Europe the melanic forms are more abundant in industrial areas than is the typical form — especially in regions of very heavy industry. Since ladybirds are dis-tasteful to predators (page 118) and make no attempt at concealment it is difficult to see how predator pressure can be the selective agent.

Since the introduction of smoke-free zones the melanics have decreased. In Birmingham, where the level of atmospheric smoke pollution fell by half between 1962 and 1966, the frequency of melanics was also approximately halved.[3,4]

Clearly the advantage of melanism in the case of the ladybird does not lie in crypsis. There is presumably a physiological advantage under conditions of atmospheric pollution, and in this case it cannot be directly related to the deposition of poisonous substances on leaves, since ladybirds are carnivorous.

The introduction of smoke-free zones has already produced a significant decrease in the proportion of melanic forms of moths in industrial areas. That is presumably associated with the change in cryptic advantage, algae and lichens having begun to replace soot on the trees.

Whilst the maintenance of polymorphism in industrial melanic moths is still generally accounted for on grounds of heterozygous advantage an alternative, and speculative, suggestion has been raised by Bishop and Cook who suggest that density-dependent selection at varied resting sites may be important.[5] Clearly if a locality has a variety of resting sites, some of which are covered in lichen and others not, competition for resting sites might be sufficient to maintain polymorphism without calling upon heterozygous advantage. Such a mechanism would be suitable for a species which travelled but little: if one colour form tended to increase some of its members would use the 'wrong' resting site and succumb readily to predators. It could also apply to a species such as the peppered moth whose individuals fly sufficiently to travel through areas of different degrees of pollution. Bishop and Cook make the point that more research is needed on the moth's high migration rate and on its population density. The fact that even in the most polluted area of Manchester the melanics never completely supplant the light forms can, perhaps, be accounted for by migration of light forms into the area.

Many insects combine cryptic colouration with 'flash' colouration which is more obviously a kind of communication since it actively misleads a predator. For example the red and yellow underwing moths (*Catocala nupta* and *Triphaena pronuba*) are nocturnal fliers but rest by day in exposed situations where they may be disturbed. Moths rest with their wings folded roof-wise over their abdomens (Figure 5.1) and the upper surface of the underwing's fore-wing is cryptically coloured. Once disturbed into flying their cryptic colouration no longer serves as protection, so they have given up any pretence of concealment in flight by evolving brightly coloured hindwings which, together with darting flight, make them positively conspicuous. Predacious birds pursue them, but when they land and quickly fold their wings the birds are unable to locate them; it is like a bird-watcher trying to find a skylark which has just landed after advertizing its presence in the air. This kind of protection is of most value to diurnal insects which live in exposed situations — namely herbivores and the surface-dwelling predators. Shorthorn grasshoppers display it prominently. Their hind-wings are large, and may be brightly coloured red or blue with brown markings breaking up the other colours. At rest the hind-wing is covered by the cryptically coloured fore-wing. When disturbed the insects make a flying leap, usually in a fairly straight line, long enough for the human eye (and presumably that of a bird) to lose track of them. Not all grasshoppers, and none of the British ones, display this feature, but rely for protection on crypsis and the fact that where they occur they tend to be present in rather large numbers. When disturbed many jump or fly in different directions which helps to confuse the predator. Any one who has tried to catch them will have learned the need for concentrating his attention on one individual at a time

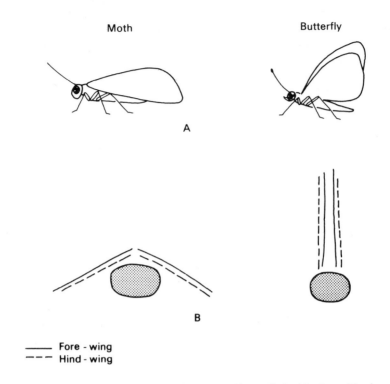

Moth   Butterfly

A

B

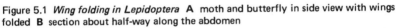

———— Fore - wing
– – – Hind - wing

Figure 5.1 *Wing folding in Lepidoptera* **A** moth and butterfly in side view with wings folded **B** section about half-way along the abdomen

and not letting himself be tempted to go after another whose flight-path happens to cross that of the first. Since species both in Britain and elsewhere lack flash colouration we may wonder how necessary it is for escaping from predators or whether it plays a part in keeping the members of the local population together at mating time, as an adjunct to the chirping, but this is pure speculation.

The praying mantises, which are readily eaten by birds, also have coloured hind-wings. As they are rather larger insects their passage through the air is easier to detect than that of the grasshoppers and they presumably derive benefit from the ability to deceive. When stationary their cryptic colouration serves them well, in fact they were used in a classic early experiment on natural selection in which the predation by birds on green and brown forms, when placed on matching and contrasting backgrounds, was recorded.

A deception which is widely used by the diurnal Lepidoptera is to draw the predator's attention to the edge of the wing area, by means of some prominent mark, so that it strikes at the wing rather than at the body. Birds and lizards can be misled in this way. Lepidoptera are over-provided with wing area and can afford to lose much of it before flight is seriously impaired. Figure 5.2 shows two examples of British butterflies which have such target areas. The most striking example is perhaps the peacock, *Nymphalis io,* which has very large and multicoloured eye-spots on both front and hind-wings — but it cannot be reproduced adequately in a

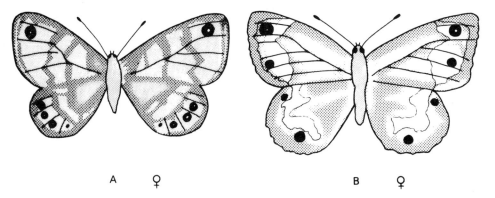

Figure 5.2 *Examples of butterflies with eye-spots on their wings* **A** Wall **B** Grayling

black and white illustration. A classic case is that of the grayling, *Eumenis semele,* which is a characteristic member of the heathland and downland fauna and therefore has to survive in an environment which offers a minimum of cover for a large insect. In flight the eye-spot protects the body from attack by birds. If it settles near the ground it may be attacked by lizards: immediately on landing it leaves the eye-spot exposed so that it may be 'safely' attacked if a predator should be present and, if no danger exists, it then conceals the front-wing behind the rear-wing whose underside, as in many butterflies, is cryptically coloured. By tilting itself towards the sun the butterfly is able to cast minimum shadow and becomes very well concealed. Dr E.B. Ford mentions an observed instance of a lizard attacking a small heath, *Coenonympa pamphilus,* in the way we have just described.[6]

Aposematic colouration

Some species of insects are hardly ever attacked by birds either because their bodies are too hard or, more often, on account of an offensive taste or because they possess a sting. It pays such insects to advertize their unpleasantness by means of some obvious signals.

In some cases the insect is acceptable for swallowing but inflicts after-effects on the predator on account of toxic substances. Birds have to learn what they may safely eat, and there is evidence that they have good memories; good enough for them to remember in the spring what they last experienced during the previous summer. Birds have colour vision, and when flying hunt mainly by sight: consequently they associate noxious prey with its general colour and markings.

Warning signs of that kind are called aposematic, and are not confined to colouration but include behaviour. Examples occur in many Orders especially amongst insects whose mode of life requires them to spend much of their time in the open. The phenomenon has evolved because it is biologically economical. Bees and wasps can protect themselves up to a point by means of their stings, but stings were evolved primarily for use against other insects and existed before the

evolution of fast-flying insectivorous birds. The word protection can be misleading
if it is taken to mean safeguarding the life of the individual insect. A bee's wings
beat very fast (200 beats per second), and are not visible in flight, but the body is,
and becomes the target — the reverse of the situation in many butterflies. An
attacking bird may well kill the bee or damage it beyond recovery although it is
stung in the process. The *species* is protected because a young bird which gains
experience of being stung by a bee will come to associate the brown or blackish
and yellow markings, fast flight and buzzing sound with danger, and select other
prey in preference. Fledglings make mistakes and learn by experience. The insect
species draws special attention to itself by its aposematic features, suffers heavy
initial loss through attack by inexperienced predators and, finally, gains by being
shunned.

The black and yellow of the wasps is another obvious example, and so is the
red and black of ladybird beetles (Coleoptera: Coccinellidae). Ladybirds are
highly distasteful and rarely taken by birds. They are amongst the most frequently
seen beetles in Britain not because of their numbers but because they spend much
of their time walking on vegetation with no pretence at concealment. This habit
is associated with their diet; both larvae and adults feed extensively on aphids which
usually cluster around the delicate terminal parts of shoots. The ladybird larva
is distasteful too, and has an aposematic pattern and colouration of its own,
usually blue with yellow or purple tubercles. The larva pupates where it feeds and
the pupa too is asposematic; it is one of the few examples of pupation in the open
with utter lack of cryptic colouration — a convincing demonstration of the efficacy
of aposematic colouration.

Mimicry

Mimicry is said to exist when two or more species, which may not be closely related,
come to resemble each other in some respects and at least one species benefits from
the resemblance. The similarity is always partly morphological but often includes
features of behaviour. The striking examples are from the tropics but the phenomenon is universal since it is a product of natural selection, and many examples
occur in the British fauna. It is convenient to discuss mimicry under two headings;
Batesian and Müllerian, but the distinction is blurred and it is probably not worth
wasting much time on attaching labels; what matters is to grasp what is happening.

Batesian mimicry occurs when a species which is edible and acceptable to
predators evolves features which make it resemble a species which is distasteful
and rejected by them. The vulnerable species is known as a mimic, and the one
which it imitates as the model.

The similarity between mimic and model is confined to external features. What
is necessary is that the predator, often a bird in flight, should fail to detect the
difference. In practice the external similarity may be close on account of the
birds' visual acuity to which we referred earlier.

Since aposematically coloured insects are avoided it follows that many mimics
share the aposematic patterns: a bird in flight does not have time to carry out

a taxonomist's examination and leaves the mimic, which would be perfectly suitable as food, untouched.

In the Batesian mimicry situation a model can tolerate only a small number of mimics, for if there are many mimics they will often be taken by predators who, failing to associate inedibility with the aposematic pattern, will subsequently destroy members of the model species.

The most famous examples are found in the Lepidoptera, because the wings afford much scope for mimicry by colour. A classic example is the widespread mimicking in Africa of butterflies of the Family Danaidae to which the Monarch butterfly, *Danaus plexippus,* belongs. Danaids possess a disagreeable taste and are immediately rejected by birds. They also possess striking patterns and therefore make admirable models. Now, butterflies of the Family Papilionidae (swallowtails) are often about the same size as the danaids whose territory they share but, lacking their disagreeable taste, have evolved a large number of mimics. Females, especially, are mimetic and much more variable than the males. In each locality the various species of papilionid mimic the danaid species which is most abundant locally. In Figure 5.3 we see a male of *Papilio dardanus,* a highly mimetic species which

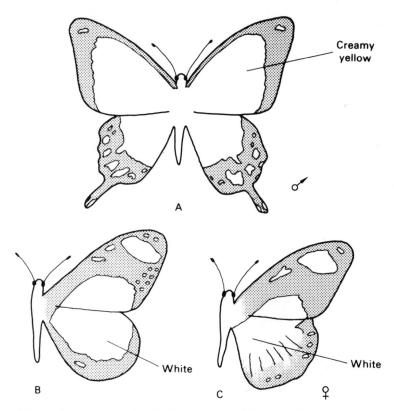

Figure 5.3 *Batesian mimicry* **A** *Papilio dardanus:* typical form. **B** Model : *Amauris niavius* **C** Mimic : *Papilio dardanus*

occurs over much of Africa and in Madagascar. It looks very much like the
European species of swallowtail, having the characteristic projections on the
hind-wings. The males of this species vary hardly at all over the entire range.
Females of the typical form, however, occur only in Ethiopia and Madagascar:
elsewhere they mimic unpalatable models and always lack the hind-wing projections.
The principal model is the danaid *Amauris niavius,* in which the sexes are similar.
It varies slightly. The specimen shown in Figure 5.3 is characteristic of the East
and South African forms while in those from West and Central Africa the hind-
wing is dark with some white near the base. The *Papilio dardanus* females mimic
each type's colour pattern correctly, and also the characteristic danaid flight. The
females mimic other distasteful species besides *Amauris niavius* and in doing so
are able to display colour combinations as diverse as black and orange; black,
white and orange; and black with creamy yellow. The mimicry is so good that
entomologists often make wrong identifications unless they are careful; the
only way to be sure is to study the wing venation which is quite different in
the two Families.

The British fauna provides some good examples of Batesian mimicry in a
minor key (Figure 5.4). The wasp beetle, *Clytus arietis,* mimics the social wasps
(Figure 5.6). The wasp beetles are longhorns (Cerambycidae) most of which,
unlike the wasps, are not very fast walkers. The colour pattern, although black
and yellow, is far from being an exact copy of a wasp's. In practice, however,

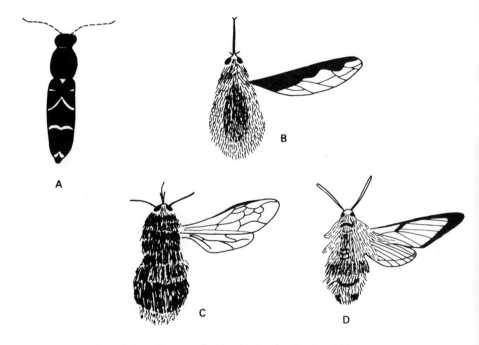

Figure 5.4 *Batesian mimicry* **A** a wasp beetle **B** a bee-fly **C** a bumblebee
D a broad-bordered bee hawk moth

the mimicry is much better than one might expect from comparing museum specimens. The beetle is usually found on the trunks of standing trees, a situation in which insects are highly vulnerable to attack by birds. It keeps its long antennae moving and swings its abdomen to right and left in a manner which, to the human eye, certainly gives a wasp-like impression. We see how an insect can mimic a totally unrelated model by making use of a combination of suitable morphology with appropriate behaviour. A wasp's antennae are shorter than the beetle's but, being somewhat clubbed and black in colour, are very noticeable in the living insect; the beetle makes use of its long antennae in imitation. Grounded wasps fold their wings longitudinally over the abdomen, giving it a parallel-sided appearance and partially obscuring the pattern of stripes; the general shape of a longhorn's abdomen resembles a wasp's more than does that of many of the more rounded beetles and the wasp's rocking motion is imitated by the beetle. That the deception would probably not succeed in flight does not matter much since longhorns spend little time in the air; the mimicry serves its purpose.

Bumblebees are obvious models since their size and stings give them considerable protection. They have been imitated by a family of Diptera, the Bombyliidae, and by two families of moths. Here again behaviour has come to the support of morphology. A few scattered hairs are characteristic of the Diptera, but in the bee-fly, *Bombylius,* the entire body is clad in a thick pile so coloured, in dark brown with paler brown around the sides and 'tail', as to resemble a certain species of bumblebee. The proboscis has been greatly extended (but note the small bifurcated labellum which reveals its true nature) to serve as a tube for sucking nectar and the bee-fly is equipped to perform the bumblebee's biological function as a pollinator. To the human eye studying a preserved specimen the resemblance to a bumblebee is still not convincing: the antennae are quite different and, most important, there is but one pair of wings instead of two. Now, the wasp beetle was able to use its long antennae to mimic the wasp because it needed protection in a fairly static condition, on tree trunks. The bee-fly gets away with having short ones because it needs protection in flight and when it is resting on flowers in the act of sucking nectar; in flight antennae are, in any case, not noticeable and when feeding a bumblebee's head is concealed in the flower so that the absence of long antennae in the bee-fly is again no source of danger. More significant is the difference between dipteran and hymenopteran wings. Bumblebees' wings are translucent but of a smoky brown shade, especially the fore-wings whose leading edge is further darkened by a strongly marked vein. The bee-fly imitates these effects successfully by means of the darkened area along the leading edge of the wing.

The broad-bordered bee hawk moth (Sphingidae) similarly darkens part of its wings, whilst it has lost the scales over most of their surface so that the venation is visible — a most unusual feature in a lepidopteran. The newly-emerged imago has wings covered in scales, most of which are then shed. The actual distribution of dark colour is puzzling since it does not match that of the bumblebee, but in practice the device is convincing. This moth mimics bumblebees of a different species from the bee-fly's model, having a different colour pattern, but again the main illusion is conveyed by long scales which imitate the body hairs of the bumblebees.

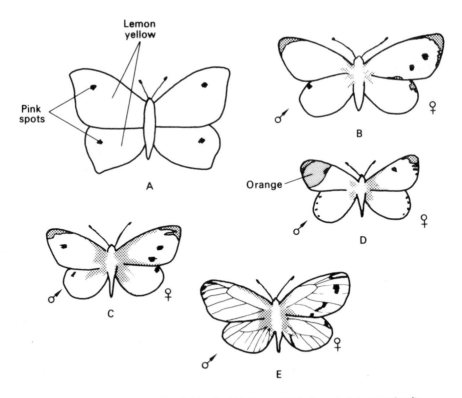

Figure 5.5 *Some pierid butterflies (whites) which form a Müllerian mimicry complex* (in dorsal view) **A** Brimstone **B** Large white **C** Small white **D** Orange tip **E** Green-veined white. The shading represents greenish-black unless otherwise stated. Sexual differences indicated; male left, female right.

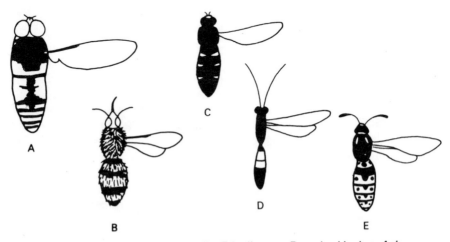

Figure 5.6 *Müllerian complexes* **A** drone-fly, *Eristalis tenax* **B** worker hive bee, *Apis mellifera* **C** a hover-fly **D** an ichneumon fly **E** social wasp. **A** and **B** based on brown and black aposematic patterns; **C D** and **E** based on yellow and black aposematic patterns

Müllerian mimicry occurs when one or more aposematic models are mimicked by species which are not necessarily as noxious as the models, or possibly not noxious at all. The result is a complex of species which benefit collectively from the resemblance because predators avoid the general pattern and the net loss from any one species is reduced; as Ford puts it, 'a single lesson of inedibility' has 'as wide an application as possible'. Evidently the system has its limits; the existence of too many mimics which possess only slightly noxious properties will reduce the efficacy of protection because a predator, having failed to learn the lesson from them, will try for the same kind of prey again and again until it does. On the other hand the existence of some less noxious members of the complex is not harmful because by increasing the size of the 'pool' from which inexperienced birds will pick their prey they reduce the number of first attempts inflicted on the highly unpalatable species. As we shall see below, even a wholly palatable species can be protected by its membership of the complex, in which case the situation approaches that of Batesian mimicry.

Good examples of Müllerian mimicry are rare in the British fauna, but one has recently been described by Marsh and Rothschild amongst the white butterflies of the Family Pieridae (Figure 5.5).[7] The large white, *Pieris brassicae,* is the lynchpin of the complex. It is highly distasteful to most birds in the adult and later larval stages, and especially in the pupal stage. It is also toxic in these stages, as was demonstrated by making intraperitoneal injections of them into mice; pupae killed the mice in ten to fifteen hours, the 5th instar larva and the female adult in thirty hours and the male adult in four days. Such tests have to be treated with caution, for similar results were not obtained with other experimental animals and of course it does not follow that the distastefulness of the insect is necessarily associated with its toxicity. It is clear, however, that most birds, the great tit being an exception, avoid eating adults and pupae of the large white. In keeping with its distasteful properties all stages of the life history are aposematic.

The small and green-veined whites, *Pieris rapae* and *P. napi,* and the orange tip, *Anthocharis cardamines*, are also distasteful as adults but much less so than the large white while the brimstone, *Gonepteryx rhamni,* as far as we know is neither distasteful nor toxic at any stage. The distastefulness of the Pieridae is the result of their larval feeding habits, the taste being due to substances present in the food plant – presumably mustard oils from various species of Cruciferae. The brimstone stands slightly apart from the other four species taxonomically, it is in a different Sub-Family, and its larva feeds not on crucifers but on buckthorn, *Rhamnus catharticus.*

Observation of the occurrence of these butterflies shows how the protective complex works. The brimstone is the first to appear, at a time when not many insects are on the wing so that one would expect it to be avidly taken by birds, but it is not. The large white appears next, soon followed by the small white. Later the green-veined white and orange tip appear and are the most numerous until subsequent broods of large and small whites emerge. The large and small whites are still to be found in the late summer. Marsh and Rothschild suggest that the brimstone owes it immunity to the unpleasant memory of the large white (and to a lesser extent of the small white) which the predators have retained from the previous season. The resemblance between the brimstone and the large white is not close, but it is perhaps close enough for the birds not to take a chance. It is difficult to account for the brimstone's immunity on any other score. A factor which reinforces the protection is that by early May there are few nestling birds ready to fly. If there were they would discover the brimstone's acceptability, as do captive birds. The existence of a wholly palatable species like the brimstone in a Müllerian complex is probably exceptional. The appearance of the large white before the remaining members of the complex is important because the inexperienced nestlings learn their lesson quickly and effectively on the most distasteful species. For the remainder of the season predation of each member species of the complex is lower than it would be if it did not occupy the same geographical area.

Another British example is Müllerian mimicry by hover-flies (Family Syrphidae, page 33) of the hive bee and wasps Figure 5.6. The drone-fly, *Eristalis tenax,* with its brown and black markings bears a resemblance to the hive bee which is much closer in nature than it looks on paper owing to the hover-fly's darting and hovering flight, and buzzing sound. *Eristalis* is often preyed on by birds and it is probably distasteful since it is very common and, were it acceptable prey, would weaken the hive bee's aposematic defences. A large number of hover-flies, ichneumons and wasps probably constitute another complex. The wasps are protected by their stings and advertize themselves by prominent black and yellow markings. The hover-flies are to a certain extent distasteful and are very numerous: many have black and yellow markings. From the illustration the resemblance to the wasp may not seem compelling, but it must be remembered that there is a whole range of colour patterns so that the prospective predators faced with fast-moving black and yellow insects learn to leave them alone. It is not clear to what extent the ichneumons form part of the complex — they certainly share the colour patterns but their body shape is quite different and there is not much evidence about their palatability. It is clear from the illustrations that the resemblance of mimic to model is greater in the case of Batesian than of Müllerian mimicry. That is only to be expected since the essence of the former case is deception — if the predator takes the mimic the lesson is partially lost — whereas in the latter case it is suggestion — the predator will learn its lesson even if the mimic be taken.

Social life

True social organization is confined to the Hymenoptera and the Isoptera which possess castes, different forms of the species which perform particular functions within the community and respond to its needs. In such social insects the offspring co-operate with their parents in the rearing of their sibs (brothers and sisters, or individuals of identical parentage). Colonies of social insects are often of considerable durability, providing protection and continuity which cannot otherwise exist amongst animals with such a short life span. Clearly sociality confers benefits: it is surprising that it has not evolved more often. So radical a development must have called for certain preconditions. It has been suggested that the ancestral termites may have adopted an early form of social life by reason of their feeding habits. Termites are xylophagous (wood-eating) but do not secrete cellulose-digesting enzymes; instead some of the most primitive ones possess a gut fauna of trichonymphs (flagellate protozoans) which provide the necessary enzymes, a classic example of symbiosis. Each generation of termites has to be repopulated with trichonymphs from the environment, for they are not transmitted by generation. Termite societies may have started by the exchange of flagellates between individual termites, a process which has evident survival value. Whilst this cannot be proven there is circumstantial evidence. Termites resemble the primitive Dictyoptera in structure, the primitive termite *Mastotermes* resembling the dictyopteran *Cryptocercus* which has symbiotic flagellates in its gut and passes them on to its young by proctodeal feeding. In the case of termites, then, it seems that the establishment of the feeding community may have evolved before social care of the brood.

In the Hymenoptera the reverse certainly occurred: social care of the brood preceded the evolution of the colony with its functionally and morphologically differentiated castes. We can form some idea of the path along which social life evolved by considering the more primitive forms which exist today. Sociality has evolved separately amongst the ants, wasps and bees. The brief outline of the increasing degree of sociality which follows, and the summary in the table overleaf, do not imply an evolutionary series but indicate the probable, general course of events in the bees.

In the solitary bees, which constitute the vast majority of Apoidea, the male dies soon after mating and the female looks for a nesting site in some hollow where she makes a few cells and fills them with a nutritious material, not honey, which she regurgitates from her crop. She then oviposits in each cell and seals it with a membranous material. The eggs hatch into larvae which feed on the stored food and pupate in the cell. The adults which emerge from the pupae escape through the seal and leave the nest, quite independently of each other and without ever having had contact with their mother. The only maternal care has been the original filling of the cells with food material, a system known as mass-provisioning since the food is provided on a once and for all basis.

A great advance in the degree of maternal care occurs in the Andrenidae. These include species which make their nests in the ground, usually on a sandy bank, facing south because sand is easy to excavate and warms up quickly in the spring. Suitable sites are often exploited by large numbers of these bees, sometimes over a succession of years, but the 'colonies' so formed are not analogous to those of the social Hymenoptera: they occur merely because the physical conditions are suitable. Some species of *Halictus* use progressive instead of mass provisioning, that is to say the female places food in the larval cells at intervals during the larva's development and then seals the cells. Advanced maternal care amongst the solitary bees is shown in *Halictus malachurus* which, however, relies on the primitive method of mass provisioning. The female excavates a burrow, often close to those

	Solitary bee	Halictus malachurus	Bombus	Family Meli- ponidae	Apis
Food storage in the nest	None	None	A little	Much	Much
Duration of the colony	No colony	Annual	Annual, but may be peren- nial in sub- tropical areas	Perennial	Perennial
Size of the colony	No colony	About twelve workers	Not more than 400 workers		Up to 60 000 workers
Differentia- tion into castes	None	Some morpholo- gical differ- ence between queens, work- ers and males	Marked differences	Marked differ- ences	Strongly marked morphological differences
Versatility of the queen	No queen	Can perform all workers' tasks	Can perform all workers' tasks		Exclusively reproductive
Feeding of the larvae	Mass provision- ing	Mass provision- ing	Progressive provisioning	Mass provison- ing	Progressive provisioning
Occurrence of swarming	None	None	None in Britain but occurs in sub-tropical areas	Yes	Yes

of other individuals, with many larval cavities leading away from it, and lays an egg in each mass-provisioned cavity. The first adults to emerge from these cavities are small sterile females which look very unlike their mother. They function as workers, and the foundress of the nest is a simple type of queen. The workers now take over the construction of more brood cells and they forage for nectar and pollen with which to provision them. The queen continues as the only egg layer, and no longer performs any other function. In late summer normal females (which resemble the queen) and males emerge from the brood cells, and mate: the fertilized females do not perform any work for the family, they visit flowers to feed themselves but use the nest merely as a shelter. In the autumn the entire population dies except for the fertilized females which remain in the nest during the winter and renew the cycle by making nests of their own in the spring. At this level, then, there is some degree of division of labour but not much care of the brood and little colony integration.

The bumblebees (Bombidae) go much further. The queen becomes active in the spring and, making a small nest in a shallow hollow in the ground constructs a few cells, lays several eggs in each and feeds the larvae progressively. The first new adults to emerge are sterile females, or workers, which take over the tasks of nest building, foraging and caring for the larvae from the queen which becomes exclusively an egg layer. Not all the cells are brood cells; the workers treat some as food storage places, but the amount which is stored is small. In later summer fertile females (potential queens) and males (drones) are produced, and mating takes place. For the rest of the summer the new queens and the drones use the nest as a shelter but contribute nothing. Later all members of the nest die, and the new queens find suitable places in which to spend the winter. The bumblebees, then, show several features of social organization which are more advanced than those of *Halictus malachurus:* there are marked differences between the castes, some food is stored in the nest and progressive provisioning of the larval cells occurs; the colony is much larger and, in the warmer countries, may last for many years so that new colonies are founded from the perennial one by several members departing from it in a swarm.

The tropical Family Meliponidae are rather more highly developed as social insects for they store a large amount of food in their nests, which are perennial. They found new colonies by swarming but, in their use of mass provisioning for the larval cells they are less evolved than the bumblebees. That is a phenomenon which should not surprise us: we cannot expect to find in nature a nice tidy series of levels of specialization towards a particular way of life because evolution is a branching, not a linear, process. No one group will display all the features which we should like to see in it in order to 'prove' our point. All we can say in this case is that on the whole, the Meliponidae have come closer to the honey bee's acme of social organization than have the Bombidae.

We shall not consider in detail either the honey bee's social organization or the morphological features which have made for their success. Suffice it to say that the honey bee's social organization is marked by pronounced morphological caste differences, progressive provisioning of the larval cells, the large size and perennial nature of the colony from which others are founded by swarming – and by the total specialization of the queen whose function is exclusively reproductive. She plays no part in the routine duties of nest building, brood care, foraging and defence of the hive, which are the task of the workers.

The termites display a completely different type of social organization. Whereas the hymenopteran colony is primarily female with males functioning only for a very short time, and exclusively as sexual partners, the termite colony is bisexual at every level. The actively reproducing members are a king and queen, often the founders of the colony, and the remainder of the members, their offspring, are either immature forms without developing wing-pads (larvae) or have differentiated into workers and soldiers which, genetically, may be of either sex but have lost the capacity for reproducing. The later larvae develop wing-pads and are then known as nymphs: they retain their potential as sexual forms and in the event of the death of the royal couple can develop as replacement reproductives. The correct balance of numbers of each caste depends on the colony's needs and there is evidence that pheromones are involved in suppressing the development of nymphs into winged sexual forms and replacement reproductives until the colony needs them, and in keeping the right proportion of soldiers to workers. The circulation of pheromones is enhanced by the exchange of food which takes place between workers, and also between workers and the royal couple and the soldiers which are unable to feed themselves. Furthermore there is mutual body licking by the workers, who also eat faeces.

Since there are over 1700 species of termites, and great differences between the morphology, behaviour and social organization of the more primitive and the most advanced forms, any brief comment about them must be in general terms. The account which follows is probably not strictly true of any species, but fairly true of many.

A termite colony is founded by a winged pair which come together during a swarming flight. After landing together they shed their wings by shaking them violently in such a way that they split off along planes near the base. They then seek a suitable site for nest building, usually a bare patch of soil, or, in the case of the dry-wood termites, a log or exposed timber on a building. Together they excavate a burrow, using their mandibles, and form a bridal chamber in which they mate and raise the first brood. During that time they do not feed but rely on the reserves of fat which they built up before leaving their original nest and also on material derived from the degenerating wing muscles: the more primitive species feed on wood while the brood is being raised. Once the first generation of workers is sufficiently developed they forage for food and also feed the royal couple which cease to feed themselves. The queen becomes enormous by enlargement of her abdomen, becoming exclusively an egg-laying machine, and the king merely refertilizes her at intervals.

The colony may be considered as being held in a persistent juvenile condition, be means of inhibitory pheromones which are secreted by the reproductives. The nature of the queen pheromone was revealed by an experiment in which a queen was held in position as shown in Figure 5.7. Colony A on one side of the screen had access only to her head and thorax, Colony B only to her abdomen. Colony A gave rise to replacement reproductives but B did not, suggesting that the abdomen produced an inhibitory substance. Covering the abdomen with shellac showed that the substance did not have to pass through the cuticle. It comes out of the anus, with the faeces, and is transmitted through the colony in the course of body licking and food sharing. Removal of the king and queen even for only twenty four hours permits nymphs in their final instars to become replacement reproductives. These forms are sexually mature but wingless: in other words they are neotenics, sexual forms in a larval body. They should be regarded as emergency reproductives only, to tide the colony over a difficult period when a normal re-

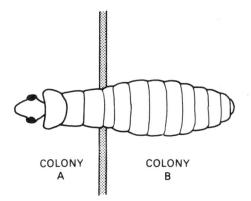

COLONY   COLONY
   A   B

Figure 5.7 *Queen termite in position for pheromone experiment*

productive dies. Since the reproductive capacity of the replacement reproductives
is much lower than that of normal founders they are allowed to exist in larger
numbers.

The replacement reproductives produce sex-specific inhibitory pheromones,
that is to say the male's inhibits the production of further male replacements and
the queen's that of females. In addition the male reproductive releases a pheromone
which stimulates the production of females.

The nest remains underground, while the workers forage and bring food back to
it. In the more primitive termites there is not a true worker caste and the worker
force is composed simply of larvae, but in the highest forms true workers exist in
the sense that they are morphologically and behaviourally distinct from the unmodified larvae and undergo no further growth or ecdysis. After sufficient larvae have
differentiated as workers, soldiers are produced in much smaller numbers: they
usually constitute about five per cent of the colony. Almost all termite species
however, have a true soldier caste which has a highly specialized morphology and
behaviour. In some species there may be two types of soldier, a smaller one which
functions within the nest and a larger one: if a breach is made in a mound the
large soldiers fill it while workers repair it. The number of larvae which differentiate
as soldiers is governed by the size of the colony and the number of soldiers which
already exist. The presence of soldiers inhibits the formation of more, as has been
shown by removing the only one from a new colony whereupon a replacement was
quickly allowed to form. Similarly the introduction of soldiers from another colony,
of the same species, will slow down the production of soldiers, which suggests that
an inhibitory pheromone is involved. The physiology of this process is not clear,
but it is known that in one primitive species an extract of the corpora allata (which
secrete the juvenile hormone) when injected into late nymphs causes them to
become soldiers, and so does an extract of the corpora allata of reproductives. It
has been suggested that the juvenile hormone, in large quantities, blocks the path
towards reproductive development and so leads to soldier production. It is likely
that pheromones secreted by the reproductives stimulate the soldiers' corpora allata

to increased secretion, which would account for the fact that soldiers are rapidly produced in young colonies.

The winged reproductives develop from last stage nymphs several months before the swarming flight. When swarming occurs the winged forms temporarily reverse their usual strong negatively phototactic behaviour and emerge in vast numbers by day, though some species are nocturnal swarmers.

In the tropics the colonies remain active throughout the year, but the nature of the activity changes. Winged forms develop from nymphs about a month before the rains begin and swarming occurs. The higher termites usually confine their swarming to a short period, whereas the more primitive ones may swarm over several months. It is thought that the mechanical effect of rain hitting the mounds acts as the stimulus for swarming. In temperate climates swarming is probably related to temperature. During the winter the colonies are reproductively inactive; the formation of winged reproductives occurs in the summer and swarming in the autumn.

Space does not allow discussion of the many types of nest which termites build. Figure 5.8. shows a typical mound of the Macrotermitidae which are the most advanced of all termites and build the largest nests. The nest began, as always, underground but as the colony increased it was gradually elevated. A mound of this type is constructed of soil particles cemented with saliva and in the middle of it lies the royal cell surrounded by *fungus gardens*. Below the mound many subterranean galleries extend into the surrounding area and permit the workers to forage for wood and other vegetable matter which is placed in the fungus gardens where it is broken down by fungal action. These termites do not possess a gut fauna of trichonymphs, but the products of the fungus gardens form the colony's main food. The walls of such a mound may be 60 cm thick and pierced by not many galleries, so that the interior is well insulated from the effects of the external temperature and the termites enjoy a high degree of homeostasis. The structure presents two problems: the metabolic activity of a great many insects in a confined space tends to raise the temperature excessively and also calls for a system of gas exchange in order to aerate the living space even though these termites can tolerate a high concentration of carbon dioxide. The sides of the mound are not smooth but fluted so that it has a buttressed appearance. The right-hand side of the main figure in Figure 5.8 shows such a buttress in sectional view. Within each buttress lies a duct, close under the surface and connected top and bottom to the air space which surrounds the main living volume of the nest. The air is hottest in the middle of the living space and heat is lost to the atmosphere from the duct in the buttresses. Convection currents are consequently set up and air containing a high proportion of carbon dioxide is exchanged for oxygen across the thin wall.

The termites' high level of social organization requires that the members be able to communicate. Not much is known about this, and it has been studied in very few species. Pheromones are used by foragers for trail laying. The trail layer moves with its abdomen pressed against the ground and then nudges other termites into activity whereupon they follow the trail. Sound signals have long

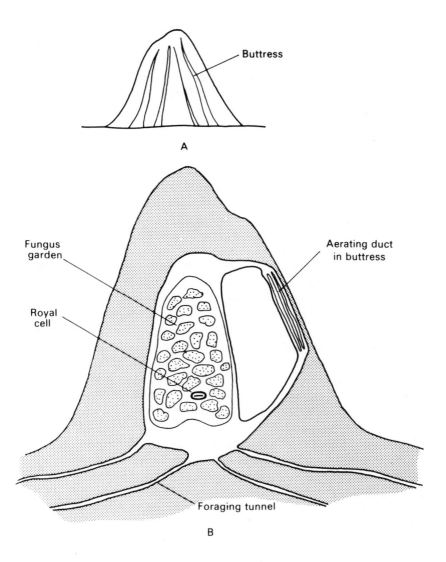

Buttress

A

Fungus garden

Aerating duct in buttress

Royal cell

Foraging tunnel

B

Figure 5.8 *A nest of Macrotermitidae* **A** external view of a mound **B** vertical section

been associated with termites. It seems likely that the tapping noise made in the galleries is an alarm signal. A sound of high intensity is produced by soldiers when they flex their heads up and down, tapping against both roof and floor of the gallery. Larvae and nymphs tap downwards only, and produce sound of low intensity. There seems to be no coding for the pattern of sound does not vary. The sound receptors are on the legs, and respond under experimental conditions to vibrations at the same rate as the taps. It is known that if the substratum is vibrated termites tend to move downwards, away from the light, and seek the shelter of crevices even more than they usually do: they also tend to aggregate. Tapping may therefore be a kind of alarm signal which has survival value. Nothing resembling the complexity of the hive bees' communication system has yet been identified amongst termites but it is difficult to believe that a sophisticated system does not exist. Termites lend themselves less well than do hive bees to investigation because their aversion to light precludes the use of large inspection windows in their nests.

The dominant invertebrates

A good way of grasping the dominant part which insects play in the economy of nature is to try and imagine what the world would be like without them: it is difficult to think of any terrestrial environment in which they do not play a major role. They differ from most other animals in that, apart from their function as prey, predators and scavengers they also serve as pollinators. Their disappearance would by synonymous with the decline of a large proportion of the insect-pollinated angiosperms, whilst even some of the angiosperms which can self-pollinate would suffer since most of them benefit from occasional outbreeding. Owing to the angiosperms' powers of vegetative reproduction the effect on our flora would not be immediate, nor would it necessarily be ultimately catastrophic – but it would be a radical change with great consequential effects on fauna. The effect on grassland would be negligible, whilst most forest trees in temperate zones are wind pollinated and would not be affected, but that does not apply to many of the trees in tropical forests. The greatest effect in temperate climates would be on annual plants which are very largely insect pollinated, and on the many flowering shrubs whose fruits are an important source of food for small vertebrates. The economic effect *would* be catastrophic, a point which is discussed in Chapter 6.

In nature the absence of insects as a source of food would have an immediate effect. There are many small groups of animals such as anteaters which, being highly specialized in their food requirements are dependent on insects, but on the whole they occupy minor ecological niches and their disappearance would not provoke a major imbalance in nature. On the other hand some large groups have become dependent on insects. It is difficult to see how spiders could survive in their absence. Many groups of birds are so modified as to be obligatory insectivores.

So far we have considered the negative side of dominance, namely what would happen if the insects were removed. The positive aspect is the way in which insects have managed to accommodate themselves so much to so many environments that they come into direct competition with man for resources and territory – and as parasitic vectors of disease. Until recently large areas of the earth were rendered partly uninhabitable to man, and even now it requires only a little disorganization in the normal running of a country for insect-borne disease to reveal itself, as we shall see in the final chapter. This is because man finds it almost impossible to exterminate insects, especially the offensive ones, so that given the slightest relaxation of control measures their numbers quickly build up again. Much money and effort are expended to keep these enemies in check, and in this sense insects can be said to be co-dominant with man.

References

1   HORRIDGE, G.A. (1962). Learning leg position by the ventral nerve cord in headless insects. *Proc. roy. Soc. B.* **157**, 33–52

2   For further reading on the insect/plant relationship: (especially the articles cited below)
     Insect/plant relationships, Ed. H.F. van Emden (1973). London: Royal Entomological Society.
     a   SOUTHWOOD, T.R.E. The insect/plant relationship – an evolutionary perspective.
     b   OSBORNE, D.J. Mutual regulation of growth and development in plants and insects.
     c   SCHOONHOVEN, L.M. Plant recognition by lepidopterous larvae.

3   CREED, E.R. (1966). Geographic variation in the two-spot ladybird in England and Wales. *Heredity* **21**, 57–72.

4   CREED, E.R. (1971). Industrial melanism in the two-spot ladybird and smoke abatement. *Evolution* **25**, 290–293;

5   BISHOP, J.A. & COOK, L.M. Moths, melanism and clean air. *Scientific American* January 1975.

6   FORD, E.B. (1957). *Butterflies.* 3rd Edition. London: Collins.

7   MARSH, N. & ROTHSCHILD, M. (1974). Lepidoptera tested on the mouse. *J. Zool., Lond.* **174**, 89 – 122.

The following works can profitably be consulted:

HASKELL, P.T. (Ed.) (1966). *Insect behaviour.* London: Royal Entomological Society. (This symposium contains authoritative but rather technical articles on many aspects of behaviour.)

BUTLER, E.G. (1962). *The world of the honeybee.* London: Collins. (An authoritative but very readable account of social organization.)

OWEN, D.F. (1971). *Tropical butterflies.* Oxford. (Contains valuable information on the genetics of mimicry.)

FORD, E.B. (1967). *Moths.* 2nd edition. London: Collins. (This, and *Butterflies* by the same author, are not only written by a leading authority but copiously illustrated with colour photographs of protective colouration and genetical variation.)

COTT, H.B. (1940). *Adaptive coloration in animals.* London: Methuen. (A standard work, splendidly illustrated, which covers the whole animal kingdom and deals extensively with insects.)

HOWSE, P.E. (1970). *Termites: a study in social behaviour.* London: Hutchinson.

Chapter 6
The Economic Importance of Insects

In the broad sense of their function in the cycle of nature insects are beneficial to man. Compared with the total number of insect species the pests are very few but their effect is immense, and discussion of the economic importance of insects revolves almost entirely around their harmful activities. A small number have obvious value, such as the termites which are used for food in some African countries, and some beetles and Lepidoptera which are used in making articles of jewellery and ornaments. Honey is an important article of commerce. Their greatest value, however, is as pollinators in which context the honey bee is supreme although, of course, many native insects are effective pollinators. The honey bee originated in Asia and spread throughout the Western part of the Old World, whence it was taken to America. It remains a wild insect and has never been domesticated: all that man has done in temperate climates has been to provide it with sophisticated hives in which to survive the winter. The partial domestication of the bee was originally intended to provide a ready source of honey but, in the long run, the bees' pollinating action has been of far greater value especially as human population has increased and it has become necessary to produce more food per acre of ground. In a country like Britain where the apple industry is important the native bumblebees could not provide adequate pollination, because they do not exist in sufficient numbers, whereas the highly sophisticated social organization of the honey bee ensures the necessary potential. The tree fruit industry all the world over depends on the honey bee. Most field crops do not, being self or wind pollinated, but benefit indirectly through the widespread use of clover, lucerne or other leguminous crops grown for animal feeding and for the improvement of the soil through nitrogen fixation. Clover is a good example of a plant which may be pollinated by a wide variety of insects but which, when grown on a large scale, needs the attention of bees for adequate pollination and the production of large quantities of seed. It is therefore ironical that modern large scale farming with its widespread and often indiscriminate use of insecticides should have contributed to the destruction of many honey bees as well as other useful insects, including the bumblebees, which are effective pollinators.

Insecticides

Because insects are so important economically a large part of our relationship with them consists of trying to kill them. In the pages that follow we shall see how, by studying the ecology of pest species, many measures of physical control can be devised, and in some instances of biological control too, but in the vast majority of cases control is a euphemism for direct killing. The weapons are insecticides, applied at some stage of the life cycle. It is rarely necessary or even possible, to *eliminate* a pest species: an effective insecticide has to reduce the pest population to an acceptable level. It will be useful to make some general comments on the nature and use of insecticides before we look at specific pests.

Insecticides function by disrupting some aspect of the insect's normal physiology, usually nervous co-ordination and muscular control. It is known that DDT affects the conductivity of nerve fibres; the organophosphates, by combining with acetylcholinesterase, allow acetylcholine to act without interruption at the synapses; carbamates act in a somewhat similar manner. The exact details of the ways in which the nervous system is attacked are, in most cases, still obscure. Ignorance of an insecticide's mode of action is a serious disadvantage when resistance to it arises: the practical solution is then to try a different insecticide. Most insecticides are discovered as a result of the routine testing of new organic products whose structure looks promising rather than by deliberate synthesis of a substance which is intended to attack a particular metabolic system: much trial and error is involved.

Insecticides used to be classified as stomach poisons and contact poisons but the distinction is no longer very valuable since many insecticides have been found to function in both ways. Traditionally the highly toxic arsenic compounds were used as stomach poisons against insects which bite and chew vegetation while pyrethrum was used as a contact poison against piercing and sucking insects such as aphids: the Hemiptera escape the stomach poisons because their mouthparts pass safely through the poisoned surface of the sprayed plant into the sap beneath. A contact poison is absorbed through the cuticle and can therefore be effective on any external part as well as on the ectodermal lining of the gut; an insect can absorb it by merely walking over the sprayed plant without actually feeding on it at all. Domestic insect sprays are always of this kind.

Insecticides have to be used in a form which will have maximum effect in the particular circumstances — always taking cost into consideration. Some are applied as dusts, most as sprays, while fumigants are very widely used against pests of stored products and in other confined spaces such as greenhouses.

The formulation of a good insecticide for a particular purpose is a highly technical matter. The vast majority of insecticides are used against agricultural pests, either of field crops or fruit trees. Not only must the insecticide be appropriate to the pest but it must be applied in a form which will give effective control without doing serious damage to the plants, which means that the concentration has to be nicely estimated since many insecticides are also phytocidal. Most insecticides are dispersed as sprays. The poisonous substance is powdered and sprayed as a waterborne suspension, the water being known as a *carrier*. Plants' leaves, however, tend not to retain water on their surface so that most of the insecticide drains off before it has time to act and even without necessarily wetting the entire leaf surface. Some substance has to be added which will act as a *wetting agent* to prevent immediate run-off, as a *spreader* and preferably as a *sticker*. Wetting is not synonymous with spreading, for even if the water is initially made to cover evenly the entire leaf surface it will soon break up into droplets and therefore not spread properly. Insecticidal action is thereby diminished because an insect walking across the leaf will encounter fewer particles of the poison and may not receive a fatal dose. Sticking action, too, is desirable lest rain should wash the poison away. A further problem is that the particles of poison may tend to coalesce, which will result in uneven dispersal of the poison on the plant surface. Emulsification is used to overcome this danger. Casein is an effective wetter, spreader, sticker and emulsifier. In an emulsified condition the insecticide particles are kept in suspension by the casein which forms an envelope around them and prevents them from forming clumps.

The most widely used carrier is, of course, water since it is the cheapest. For some purposes, however, an insecticide may be carried in an oil, which has the added benefit of a toxic effect of its own.

It is desirable that the toxicity of the insecticide should persist for some time after its application in order to obviate the cost of further treatment soon after the first one, and some insecticides possess this residual effect.

Many agricultural insecticides are applied as very finely powdered dusts. In order to enable them to pass properly through the dusting machinery and to ensure an even spread of dust a carrier is used. Absorptive substances such as kaolin, when mixed with an insecticide dust, release it slowly in the field, while less absorptive substances, such as talc, will release the insecticide more rapidly.

Fumigation is probably the most important method of controlling pests of stored products. A fumigant is a true gas whose molecules can penetrate the interstices within tightly packed materials. Grain in bulk or in sacks, and milled flour, are the products that are most widely treated in this way, and the most commonly used gas is methyl bromide which is non-flammable and can be used safely on most products although in the case of flour it is unsuitable and ethylene oxide is used instead. Fumigation is a potentially dangerous operation since the gases used are poisonous to man: precautions have to be taken to ensure the safe dispersal of the gas after the operation. The first essential is to seal the space that is to be treated, either a ship's hold, warehouse, silo or mill. The dose to be applied will depend on the ambient temperature and on the sorptive properties of the product, its containers and the walls of the building. These properties must be ascertained for the particular fumigant in the circumstances of its use. Fumigation is clearly a highly technical matter.

Insecticides are best classified according to their chemical composition. We shall very briefly consider some of those which are most widely used.

The *Arsenicals* have been used in various forms for a long time. Today the only one that is widely used is Paris green $(CH_3 COO)_2$ Cu. 3 Cu $(As O_2)_2$. In the form of a dust, with sulphur or hydrated lime as a carrier it has been a valuable weapon against mosquito larvae, being dusted on to the surface of large areas of water. Its use declined with the introduction of powerful synthetic insecticides, but it has come into favour again as an alternative to them since the appearance of resistant strains.

Methyl bromide, CH_3Br, is an almost all purpose fumigant since not only is it non-flammable but also highly penetrating. It is effective against all stages of the insect life history but is a slow killer. Like most fumigants it is toxic to vertebrates but slightly less so than hydrocyanic acid gas, HCN, the other widely used fumigant. HCN, being a fast killer, can be used with advantage in places which cannot be made air tight, but its toxicity and flammability render its use very dangerous.

Several substances (eg nicotine, pyrethrum and rotenone) which occur naturally in plants, or are derived from them have insecticidal properties:

Nicotine is used as a spray, a dust or a fumigant. It is highly toxic to insects and to man, but since it decomposes rapidly when exposed to the air it has no lasting environmental effect. It is used in orchards and in greenhouses under conditions which can be strictly controlled.

Pyrethrum was by far the most widely used insecticide in sprays and dusts before the Second World War. The synthetic insecticides were then developed rapidly owing to the threat of severed communication with the main sources of *Chrysanthemum cinerariaefolium* in the Far East. The great advantages of pyrethrum are its harmlessness to mammals and bird and the rapidity of its paralysing action. It is used in fly sprays on account of its rapid 'knock down' effect, and such sprays are theoretically safe even under domestic conditions since no harm is done if droplets should fall on exposed food. In practice, though, these sprays nearly always include some synthetic insecticide which produces a higher kill than pyrethrum can unless it is highly concentrated, and pyrethrum is expensive. Care should therefore always be taken not to expose food to domestic fly sprays. The great disadvantage of pyrethrum is that it decomposes rapidly on exposure to light and air, but even this fact must be balanced against its harmlessness to the environment.

Rotenone is extracted from the roots of several plants which grow mainly in Malaysia. The principal source is *Derris elliptica*, and the product is known more generally as derris than as rotenone. It is used with spray oils (see below) to enhance their insecticidal effect, and as a dust. It is more toxic to man than pyrethrum but is safe in the proportions in which it is used. It acts less quickly than pyrethrum against insects but has greater residual effect.
Spray oils are used either with or without the addition of other insecticides. The paraffin (kerosene in the USA) fraction of petroleum distillates, or emulsions of highly refined lubricating oils, are widely used in the USA against pests of fruit trees. In Europe coal tar derivatives, tar oils, are often used especially as winter washes on deciduous trees in the leafless condition.

The lethal action of these oils is partly physical, by suffocation, and partly chemical. Spray oils are effective against many insects including aphids and scale insects (Hemiptera: Coccidae) which are serious pests of citrus trees.

The *Chlorinated hydrocarbons* (Figure 6.1) came into use during the Second World War when DDT was used widely as a spray in mosquito infested areas and as a dust for anti-louse treatment of clothing. Their residual effect, which is far greater than

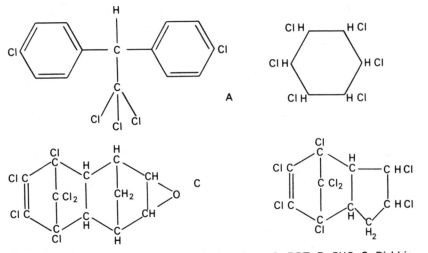

Figure 6.1 *Structure of some chlorinated hydrocarbons* **A** DDT **B** BHC **C** Dieldrin
D Chlordane

that of any of the natural insecticides, has been a mixed blessing. It has made possible the long-term treatment of buildings against mosquitoes, resulting in economy and enabling workers in the field to give protection to many more people than would have been the case with say, pyrethrum. In the early days mass spraying or dusting of areas of bush was practised from the air. The chlorinated hydrocarbons are, however toxic to man and other animals when they accumulate, as they do, in the soil and to some extent in plant tissue. Milk from cows which have fed on treated herbage may contain unacceptable quantities of the insecticides which have adverse effects on the human liver, kidney and heart. In addition although they act slowly they are very powerful and indiscriminate, so that their use results in the death of many valuable predacious insects, bees and birds. Their use should be carefully controlled. In Britain DDT as a domestic insecticide has been banned since 1971, and it will cease to be used on refuse tips after the end of 1975: it can still however be used for some agricultural purposes. Because of its effectiveness, however, DDT is still employed in anti-mosquito work since the potential advantages are considered often to outweigh the risk.

All the chlorinated hydrocarbons can be used as sprays, dissolved in oils or as emulsions, and as dusts: Gamma – BHC can also be used as a fumigant. The following table compares two characteristics of the principal hydrocarbons with those of

	Toxicity to insects	Residual effect
Gamma–BHC also known as Lindane or Gammexane	much greater	less
Chlordane	greater	less
Dieldrin	very much greater	greater

DDT. The practical effect of all insecticides however, depends very much on how they are used.

Wherever allusion to BHC is made in this book it refers to the gamma isomer of BHC, which is the actively insecticidal form.

The *Organo-phosphates* (Figure 6.2) are highly effective stomach and contact poisons, even better than the chlorinated hydrocarbons, whose vapour acts as a fumigant. They are also highly toxic to homiothermic animals and must be used with stringent precautions, such as protective clothing including synthetic rubber boots and gauntlets for the operators, and a respirator when the concentrate is being handled. Their residual effect is greater than that of DDT and, in addition they are effective against mites whereas the chlorinated hydrocarbons are not. On account of these properties the principal organo-phosphates, parathion and mala-thion are widely used but owing to their dangerous nature their use on fruit and vegetable crops has to be closely controlled by, for example, ensuring that enough time elapses between application and harvest for the residual effect to be dissipated.

The *Carbamates* (Figure 6.2) are comparatively modern insecticides which act as inhibitors of cholinesterase, but the effect is reversible in sub-lethal doses.

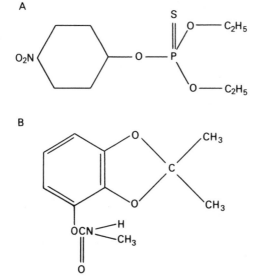

Figure 6.2 **A** Parathion, an organo-phosphate **B** Bendiocarb, a carbamate

An insecticide for the future?

Owing to the increasing concern of both the scientific and general public at the long
term effect of chlorinated hydrocarbons and organo-phosphates much research has
been devoted to the problem of finding a 'safe' and effective insecticide. Synthetic
pyrethroids may provide a solution. [1,2] Workers at Rothamsted Experimental
Station have sought to combine the low toxicity to mammals and high toxicity to
insects of pyrethrum with the residual qualities of the 'dangerous' insecticides. The
earlier synthetic pyrethroids met the toxicity requirements better than any other
insecticides but decomposed rapidly in the air and in the light. The most recent
one, permethrin (at first known as NRDC 143, having been developed under the
auspices of the National Research Development Corporation), is stable when
applied in many different forms, but safe since initial tests suggest that in mammals
it is rapidly metabolized and excreted. It is, however, highly poisonous to fish. The
substance is still at the experimental stage and its ultimate value will depend partly
on manufacturing costs. It may prove to be of very widespread application, provided
of course that the phenomenon of resistance does not prove to be a serious disadvantage.

Resistance to insecticides

The use of insecticides on a massive scale was a by product of the Second World
War when large armies had to be maintained in good health in tropical and sub-
tropical areas. The chief danger was from the mosquito-borne diseases, and also the
problem of lice which always arises when large numbers of people have to live in
close proximity and inadequate hygiene. The louse problem was met by the use of
lauryl thiocyanate under the name of Lethane, and the greater problem of mosquito control by DDT. After the war, when the world became acutely aware of the
need to increase food production, DDT came into general use as an agricultural
insecticide since it is effective against almost all insects. For a while it was thought
to be the universal panacea against insect pests, and then the phenomenon of resistance
appeared. In areas from which a mosquito species had apparently been eradicated a
population began to build up again, and quite rapidly. What had happened was that
the original population had not been totally destroyed, but merely reduced to so
small a size that the surviving individuals were inconspicuous. Natural regeneration
from the few non-susceptible individuals was rapid, especially under tropical conditions. After a few more years of reproduction, accompanied by continued attack
with DDT, the mosquito population over large areas in the tropics consisted largely
of immune individuals.

   The development of resistant strains of mosquitoes has often been the result of
the widespread use of agricultural insecticides and not of anti-mosquito measures
per se. By 1968 no less than thirty six species of *Anopheles* showed resistance to
dieldrin, fifteen to DDT and thirteen to both. One species had evolved resistance to
malathion. Experience shows that no sooner is a new insecticide put to general use
than resistance appears somewhere, and then more widely. There is no once and for
all insecticide that is safe to use.

Resistance is a genetical phenomenon, with the insecticide acting as the selective agent. Most mosquitoes in the field develop resistance to dieldrin much more rapidly than to DDT, which suggests that in the case of the former it might be due to the effect of a dominant and, in the latter, of a recessive gene. That is an instance of a dominant gene spreading rapidly through a population: we saw another one earlier in the case of melanic moths (page 113). The spread was more rapid in the case of the mosquito than in the case of the moths because of the intensity of the selective agent: whereas industrial pollution accumulated slowly insecticides came into large-scale use suddenly and the mosquitoes responded accordingly. The intensity of the selective agent accounts for the relatively rapid spread of DDT resistance in spite of its dependence on a recessive gene.

Breeding experiments in which resistants are crossed with susceptibles to produce an F_1 show that the alleles segregate on simple Mendelian lines for monohybrid inheritance. The straight dominant/recessive effect is less strongly marked in the case of DDT resistance: that is to say that whilst the double recessive is largely immune to a given dose of DDT many heterozygotes are also partly immune at the same dosage. In the case of dieldrin resistance double dominants are largely immune to a given dose but no heterozygotes are immune to the same dosage. It follows that the reservoir of genes which confer susceptibility to DDT is greater than the reservoir of those which confer susceptibility to dieldrin. In practice control depends on choosing the right insecticide for the time being: if resistance has begun to build up against one insecticide it is time to switch to another.

Problems can arise even so. *Anopheles gambiae*, a major vector of malaria, developed dieldrin resistance in East African bush country but did not lend itself well to attack by DDT for behavioural reasons. DDT has a strong irritant effect on this species which caused it to make less use of native huts as places in which to shelter, not remaining long enough to absorb a fatal dose. *An. gambiae* happens to be one of the species which, although they often enter human habitation, find equally suitable shelter out of doors.

Genetic control

As an alternative to the apparatus of control by insecticides, which is both costly and potentially harmful to the environment in general, a more insidious form of attack has been tried. A large number of males are bred, sterilized, and released into the environment. Since sterilization does not interfere with mating behaviour a large number of sterile matings occur. The method has been used successfully against the screw-worm fly, *Cochliomyia*, in the south eastern United States. As a result of the release into the environment of a very large number of sterile males the species was eradicated. This method is known as indirect control and may well be applicable to free-living insects as we shall see below. In stored products such as grain, indirect control of this type is undesirable for various practical reasons: for example, eradication cannot really succeed in warehouses which receive fresh stocks of infested grain, the introduction of sterile insects increases the total quantity of insect fragments which remain in the flour after the grain has been milled and, of course, the technique is effective only for the species to which the sterile males belong. If more than one pest species is present in the stored product it will have to be attacked separately, perhaps by a further introduction of sterile males or by fumigation.

Direct control by irradiation from an electron accelerator can profitably be used against pests of stored products: in this method the product with its contained pests is subjected to radiation which kills the pests and the disadvantages described above are obviated. It can be economic only if done on a large scale.

Control of vectors of disease in the field by using sterile males is likely to work best when the existing adult population has been reduced by insecticides: non-residual insecticides have to be used in order to avoid excessive loss of the sterilized males that are subsequently introduced. An estimate of the population newly emerged from pupae is then needed, and sufficient sterile males have to be produced to provide overwhelming competition for the local males. Theoretically the method should be appropriate in tsetse control since the numbers of tsetse are much lower than those of other pest species and fewer sterile males would have to be bred, furthermore the females mate but once though some males may do so more than once. The tsetse, however, does not breed readily in captivity and has a low reproductive rate, but the method will probably find increasing application especially since the pregnant females are highly resistant to insecticides and can be eradicated only by repeated spraying or other expensive measures (see below).

Sterility in males can be produced in the laboratory by exposing them to gamma-radiation, usually from cobalt—60. It was found that treating the pupae of tsetse resulted in high mortality but that adult males could safely be irradiated: exposure to 8000—16 000 r soon after emergence produced sterility in ninety five per cent of the sample. Adult mosquitoes have been similarly treated. Chemo-sterilization has advantages over radiosterilization, the principal one being that it can be carried out in the field which obviates the necessity of large scale laboratory breeding. It has been used against the larval stages of mosquitoes. Many chemo-sterilants, however, are toxic to mammals and resistance to them has already appeared in *Aedes aegypti*. Tsetse flies have been chemosterilized successfully as adults in the laboratory by allowing newly emerged males to walk over a glass surface treated with 10mg tepa per square foot. The same result can be achieved by spraying them and in either case the flies' subsequent behaviour is normal, but there is evidence that laboratory-bred flies, even if they are not sterile, survive poorly in the field as against native flies. Consequently attempts have been made to chemo-sterilize in the field but there are many difficulties. Since the chemosterilant is liable to become degraded under field conditions the area would have to be treated at frequent intervals which would mean releasing an undesirable amount of sterilant into the environment. Sterilants, being non-specific, would present a threat to all organisms. As an alternative to its broadcast dissemination it should be possible to introduce the sterilant into a bait host animal or by means of a bait animal to tempt the flies into a shelter which has been treated with sterilant. Difficulties still exist: the sterilant does not remain long in the mammal's blood and in any case may prove fatal to it before any flies have sucked its blood, whilst merely tempting the

flies into shelter involves a large element of chance. All the same, improved techniques may increase the usefulness of a potentially valuable method.

Another method is to exploit the F_1 male sterility which arises in some crosses
between members of closely related mosquito species. In *Anopheles gambiae* several
biological races occur, that is to say populations exist which, whilst possessing no
classical taxonomic differences (except in very slight chromosomal features), are
slightly different physiologically and ecologically. Type A prefers more humid environments than Type B, but they can occur together. When they do it is found
that the F_1 males are sterile. Crosses between males of Type A or B and females of
other closely related species have the added advantage of producing a vast prepon-
derance of males over females in the F_1. These F_1 males, in spite of their sterility,
have a greater mating propensity than do normal males: consequently such crosses
are a potential source of eggs which can be released into natural habitats.

In all probability methods of genetical control will become more important as
alternatives to insecticides with harmful environmental effects, but for practical
purposes against most insect pests they are still in their infancy.

Biological control

Owing to the undesirable environmental effects of the most potent insecticides the
idea of combatting a pest with the aid of its natural enemies is attractive. Theoretically it should also be cheaper. Unfortunately it is very difficult to achieve in practice although there have been some great successes. The control of the prickly pear
cactus in Australia by means of the moth *Cactoblastic cactorum* is a classic example. It is, however, easier to control a plant than an insect pest because the
former is static and the control can be brought to it. The biological control of insect
pests has occasionally been achieved, but it is a far more sophisticated matter than
even the use of the right insecticide technique and offers less guarantee of success.

The only effective controls on insects, that is to say the only organisms which
kill enough of them fast enough, are micro-organisms and other insects. Micro-
organisms cannot readily be made to control a particular outbreak since their own
multiplication depends on environmental conditions, especially climatic ones,
which cannot be guaranteed. Limited success has been obtained with bacterial pre-
parations against lepidopteran caterpillars and beetle larvae.

The best controls are other insects. The classic case occurred towards the end of
the last century in California. Citrus plantations were being ruined by a plant bug,
the cottony cushion scale insect, *Icerya purchasi*, which had entered the country
from Australia or New Zealand where its natural predator is a ladybird beetle
Vedalia cardinalis. Specimens of the beetle were imported and when released into
the Californian orchards completely destroyed the pest, a performance which has
been equalled wherever the process has been repeated. The very success of the
venture raised extravagant hopes for the future of biological control which have not
usually been realized, although the principle is a sound one and is likely to be
developed.

Debach gives an example of recent control which was not only a complete success but demonstrates how cheap biological control can be.[3] Citrus crops are very important to the economy of Greece and surrounding countries. Many coccids (scale insects) attack them, but in 1962 the principal one was *Chrysomphalus dictyospermi* which produced leaf-drop, dead twigs and fruit encrusted with scale. Several species of likely parasites were transported by air from the breeding houses in the University of California. One of them, a small chalcid, *Aphytis melinus* (Hymenoptera: Chalcididae), survived well under local conditions and in a couple of years had eliminated the scale at a cost of a few hundred dollars. That figure includes the cost of transporting the parasites to Greece and colonizing them there but not, of course, of maintaining the breeding establishment. By any standards the cost compares well with that of chemical control which in this case had not been particularly successful.

In the early days of biological control predators were generally introduced into the affected habitat in the hope that they would establish themselves and build their numbers up sufficiently to deal with an outbreak of the pest. That may happen, but it is asking a lot of nature for at least two reasons. First, if the predator has been introduced from abroad in sufficient quantity it may deal with the current outbreak but not be able to survive into a further generation in its new environment. Secondly, even if it does it may not appear in sufficient numbers to deal adequately with a large outbreak — phytophagous insects are usually more numerous than those higher in the pyramid of numbers. We see this phenomenon occurring in the case of ladybird beetles and aphids. Ladybird adults and larvae do consume large numbers of aphids, but that does not prevent aphids existing in numbers large enough to damage crops: in a year of large aphid numbers the predators eat more of them than in a lean year, but the percentage increase in predation is not proportional to the increase in the pest population. Consequently it may be necessary to breed large numbers of the predators in specially controlled conditions so that they may be liberated *en masse* at the appropriate time. Debach points out that the relatively minor status of biological control is not so much that it has failed as that it has rarely been tried. Of the 5000 species of known insect pests about five percent have been tackled by means of parasites or predators. Where the attempt, based on sound research, has been made the success rate has been high and the ultimate cost low. Initial costs may be high on account of the painstaking research that is needed but a successful control, once found, can usually be used in many countries and is often complete since the problem of resistant strains of the pest does not arise as it does in the case of chemical control.

The action of insects as agents of control is not limited to their effect on living organisms. In Chapter 4 we referred to the habits of dung-beetles which break up vertebrate faeces. The beetles perform a useful function in nature, helping to return to the soil materials that have been extracted from it by plants and which were subsequently assimilated by herbivores. The function is taken for granted, the various species of beetle being adapted to dealing with different types of dung. When the balance of nature is upset, however, by the introduction of a foreign species of herbivore the indigenous beetles may be unable to cope with the new type of dung so that it accumulates, preventing the proper growth of grass and encouraging the growth of undesirable vegetation. That is what happened when cattle were introduced into Australia, and the indigenous beetles, adapted to dealing with marsupial dung which is of a completely different consistency, were unable to degrade the cow pads.[4] Dung-beetles from Africa, which are adapted to disposing of the dung of large herbivores, are used as controls. Great care is taken to avoid harmful side effects of introducing foreign insect species, especially since dung-beetles are usually heavily parasitized by mites and other potentially harmful organisms. Instead of importing adult beetles the African eggs only are taken from dung balls, washed, surface sterilized and inserted into dung balls made of Australian materials in which they are allowed to complete their development. The emerging adults are then allowed to breed and in that way a 'clean' population is produced for releasing into the Australian bush. When released in sufficient quantity for them to become established they have completely solved the cow pad problem and produced no harmful side effects. Biological control is certainly a painstaking business, but not a costly one.

Insects of medical importance

Relatively few insect species are vectors of serious diseases in man and domestic animals, but their effect is out of all proportion to their number. Modern hygiene has almost eliminated them from the developed countries, but in tropical and subtropical areas trypanosomiasis, malaria and filariasis still lower the quality of life and may even be limiting influences on the development of countries.

Trypanosomiasis

This is one of the most serious diseases of tropical Africa. It is caused by protozoan parasites, trypanosomes, which are carried in the blood plasma of man and many other mammals as well as some birds and reptiles. The parasites are conveyed from one vertebrate host to another by the tsetse fly, *Glossina*. In man the disease is called sleeping sickness. In the early stages the patient suffers a fever, subsequently his face and feet become swollen and unless he is treated he will die — within a year in the case of Rhodesian sleeping sickness or, in the Gambian form of disease after several years, having perhaps gone mad meanwhile. In each form the lethargy from which the disease takes its name is evident. Other species of trypanosome, some of which can be transmitted by species of tsetse which bite man, cause the related disease of nagana in all kinds of domestic animal. Trypanosomiasis is therefore a limiting factor to the health and prosperity of the large part of Africa (Figure 6.3) over which the mean annual rainfall exceeds 500mm and which provides suitable habitats for tsetse.

The distribution of the various species of *Glossina* is controlled by temperature, humidity and vegetation. The genus is remarkably adaptable so that species are able to function effectively right up to the limit of the range and in the numerous different habitats which occur within it. Nash has described an ideal habitat for *G. morsitans*, the principal vector of Rhodesian sleeping sickness.[5] It must have

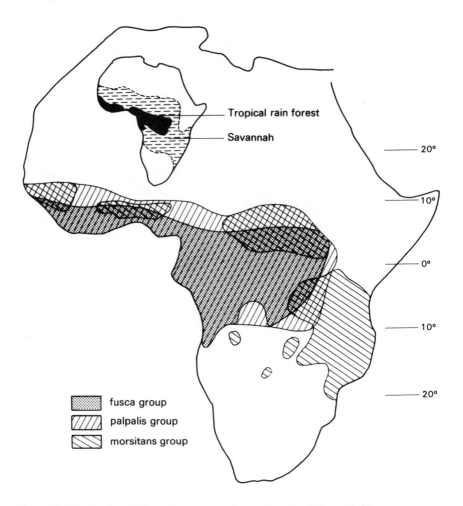

Figure 6.3 *Distribution of the various groups of tsetse* (based mainly on Nash)

enough game resident in it to provide a source of food and enough vegetation to
provide shade for the adults. In addition it must offer breeding sites which are
neither too dry nor likely to be destroyed by flooding or by fire. That is because
the hardness and humidity of the soil are very important for the survival of the
larvae and pupae. All tsetse are viviparous. The female gives birth on the ground to
a large larva (Figure 6.4) which immediately burrows into the soil where it pupates,
so that soft soil is necessary: a variety of shaded sites such as animal burrows,
rock-shaded places and tree roots are suitable. The habitat which has just been described is called by Nash a *true habitat*, one to which the species can retreat to build
up its numbers when conditions are adverse. On the other hand the flies are often
driven by a temporary shortage of food in the true habitat to venture briefly into
open areas, which Nash calls *feeding grounds*, where game is easily spotted. Having
fed, the flies return either to their true habitat or else to an intermediate one which

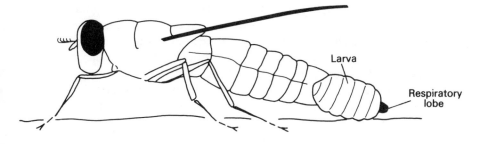

Figure 6.4 *Female tsetse giving bith to a larva*

provides enough shelter and breeding sites for most of the year although the true habitat is always resorted to when the season is adverse. It will be clear from these brief ecological comments that an understanding of the biology of a particular species is invaluable when planning control measures. It is both cheaper and more effective to direct these measures at particular habitats than to attempt a blanket control, especially in so variable a genus as *Glossina*.

The genus falls into three groups, separated on morphological characters. The members of the groups, however, also have different habitats and transmit different trypanosomes. Each group is named after the specific name of its most important member. The principal ecological features of the groups are shown very roughly in the following table.

	Fusca group	*Palpalis group*	*Morsitans group*
Habitat	Forest	Forest, swamps and riverine vegetation extending into savannah	Savannah
Disease	Nagana only	Gambian sleeping sickness	Rhodesian sleeping sickness
		Nagana	Nagana (the most important carriers)

Nagana   This occurs in all domestic animals. The most widespread trypanosome is *Trypanosoma congolense* which affects all domestic animals. *T. vivax* affects cattle, sheep and goats whilst *T. brucei* affects cattle only slightly but is highly pathogenic to most other animals including camels. The effect of the disease resembles that of sleeping sickness; swelling of extremities, anaemia, fever, wasting and general weakness followed by death. Trypanosomes are not confined to domestic animals, but exist in most forms of game both in the forest and on the savannah. They appear to have no adverse effect on the game animals which, being native to the continent have, over a long period of time, evolved a tolerance to them. Strictly speaking trypanosomes can no longer be described as parasites of game animals which are the descendants of immune individuals. The game, however, provides a reservoir of trypanosomes that can be transmitted to domestic animals which, being relatively recent arrivals, have as yet produced few resistant strains and none which are wholly immune. The problem is greatest in cattle, which are very important not only as meat and as draught animals but also as status symbols. A man's position in society often depends on the number of cattle which, provided that they are able to stand, can be used as a form of currency irrespective of their condition. In such areas there is a great temptation to control tsetse by shooting out the game, a drastic solution which has succeeded in eradicating the fly from several localities. This method, coupled with the careful use of prophylactic drugs should, theoretically, over a period of years produce healthy domestic herds. It is, however, an increasingly unpopular solution in an age which is alive to conservation and even more to the income from tourists who come to see the game.

It is possible to compromise by substituting selective for wholesale slaughter. The various species of fly differ considerably in host preference. In general Suidae (pigs) are the most favoured hosts, some species confining themselves mainly to them, but Bovidae (antelopes) are used extensively by all species. Other hosts are primates, the very large game animals and, for a few species, some birds and reptiles. Amongst the suids the warthog, bushpig, giant river hog and red river hog are used. The bushbuck is by far the most favoured bovid though many others are used. Wildebeest and zebra are never bitten (although the domestic horse is highly vulnerable) and neither are several species of small antelope. By careful study of the fly's habits in a particular area it is possible virtually to exterminate it by shooting or, in the case of very large game such as elephant and buffalo, driving out only the favoured hosts and leaving other game untouched. Accurate local knowledge is the prerequisite for all imaginative control measures.

A far more attractive idea than slaughtering game is to use the cattle country for game farming, in which case the natural hoofed mammals would be preserved and would provide a source of protein which could be cropped. Experimental game farming has already been tried, the eland antelope having proved particularly suitable, but its widespread use will deny grassland to domestic cattle and run into opposition from cattle owners – a classic case of the difficulty of introducing an imaginative idea which runs counter to tradition.

If the life cycle of the trypanosome cannot be broken by destroying its wild reservoir it can be attacked by destroying the vector. Since the tsetse has rather specialized requirements for breeding it can be attacked by reducing the vegetation which protects it from the intense heat and light. It should be sufficient to clear the relatively small areas in which all the conditions are right for breeding. That is more easily said than done, for the true habitats are not easy to identify in a large area, and even if only a few are overlooked the population may build up again. It is more easy to achieve in areas which have a severe climate and where the potential breeding sites are correspondingly few. An alternative is to strip the trees completely in a belt two miles wide around the area which is to be protected, a difficult task in thickly forested areas but feasible in savannah.

The sheer size of the tsetse area presents difficulties. The palpalis group has its home in the coastal swamps and the rain forest, but extends far out along the streams into savannah. That is because in the course of man's gradual reduction of the forest area large islands of forest were left behind: the areas of elephant grass and trees which separate the islands are known as *derived savannah*. The streams which, crossing this savannah, link the islands with the main forest area and extend beyond the derived savannah into the savannah proper form natural channels along which the tsetse find ample true habitats. Since the different species of tsetse have their specific environmental requirements a knowledge of their ecology can greatly simplify control. It is often sufficient to strip the lower branches from tall trees and eradicate the smaller shrubs along the water courses. The space thereby created will be occupied by grass, which does not provide enough shade shelter, and in addition the removal of shrub vegetation allows the stream to dry up partially during the dry season and destroys potential breeding sites. It is simpler, cheaper and less destructive to the environment as a whole to attack the riverine species of tsetse in this way than by total destruction of the vegetation. An alternative is to spray the riverine vegetation with residual insecticides which can be more economical in labour costs than the large scale clearing of vegetation, especially if it is possible to identify breeding sites and so to spray selectively.

Spraying can be employed against *G. morsitans*, the most important carrier of nagana, but it is an operation of vast proportions owing to the extent of the woodland savannah. It has been successful when ecology has been taken into account. It is not possible to make sweeping generalizations about the ecology of a species: its behaviour in one area may not be matched elsewhere. *G. morsitans* in north eastern Nigeria was found to seek shelter from the sun by resting on tree trunks just above ground level, the temperature there being just sufficiently lower than the ambient temperature not to be lethal. Consequently an operation directed at spraying the right places was effective and economical. On the other hand in Guinea, where the savannah is cooler and more humid, the fly rests on the underside of horizontal branches up to twelve feet above the ground: there the technique of spraying had to be altered accordingly.

Sleeping sickness   The remarks about *G. morsitans* in relation to nagana apply generally to its action as a vector of Rhodesian sleeping sickness. This form of trypanosomiasis differs from the Gambian form not only in running a much more rapid and lethal course but in being transmissible from animals to man by the tsetse, whereas Gambian sleeping sickness is transmitted from man to man. Under epidemic conditions, however, the Rhodesian form, too, can be transmitted from man to man especially in villages where tsetse actually breed near, or even in, the huts.

Rhodesian sleeping sickness is a disease of the East African bush, where man lives in small numbers in close contact with game: bushbuck are thought to be the principal reservoir. Since the most exposed communities are small and isolated they are unlikely to have access to early medical help, which is particularly important in this disease. Ironically a state of peace in the country has been conducive to the spread of the disease, for when tribal warfare drove men to live in large communities for safety game was frightened away from the vicinity. The disease has been controlled by encouraging a return to larger settlements and farming the area. Drugs are now available which largely cure affected cases.

Gambian sleeping sickness is essentially a riverine disease for although *G. palpalis*, its principal vector, occurs in the forest as well conditions there are less propitious for transmission from man to man than they are along the water courses which lead through the derived savannah. When the streams dry up water is restricted to occasional permanent pools, which determine the location of villages. Unfortunately these are the very places to which the tsetse must retreat in the dry season, and people cannot avoid the fly when they visit the pools to obtain water. In the forest, rivers do not dry up. Man depends on them for transport and partly for food; his settlements tend to be sited along them. On the other hand, on account of the humidity and shade, suitable tsetse habitats are widely scattered, game is plentiful and not concentrated along the rivers and individual flies travel longer distances than they do in the restrictive conditions of the savannah. Consequently the likelihood of an infected fly feeding on man is greatly reduced.

The control of Gambian sleeping sickness is undertaken in the same way as the control of *palpapis*-borne nagana, by clearing and spraying. Formerly success was obtained by moving human populations from dangerous areas to areas which had previously been made clean by the methods described above. A policy of moving people out of their home areas has an offensive flavour, however desirable it may be on grounds of health, and medical help is better. The prophylactic drug pentamidine (prophylaxis meaning prevention, as opposed to therapy meaning curing) used in conjunction with tsetse eradication has greatly reduced the incidence of the disease.

Faster means of transport present a problem in containing sleeping sickness as they do in many other diseases which take time to declare themselves. It is quite possible for an outbreak to occur in a relatively free area because of the arrival of an infected man, perhaps in search of employment. In the absence of total extermination of the fly in that area, which is almost impossible to achieve, the disease may always flare up. Consequently after the original costly eradication of the disease, maintenance of the clean conditions calls for extensive and continuous survey and testing over large areas of difficult country. It puts a heavy charge on the shoulders of poor countries.

Chagas' disease   There is one other form of human trypanosomiasis which occurs only in Mexico and the northern two thirds of South America. The parasite is *Trypanosoma cruzi*, and the vectors are several species of blood-sucking bugs (Heteroptera: Reduviidae) including *Triatoma* and *Rhodnius*. Man is not the only vertebrate host: domestic dogs and cats and many small wild mammals, such as armadillos and monkeys, some of which live in proximity to human dwellings harbour the parasite which is therefore extremely difficult to eradicate. *T. cruzi* is not strictly speaking a blood parasite although the stage of its cycle which is sucked up by the vector is spent in the blood: for most of the time it is intracellular in the cardiac muscle and the reticulo-endothelial system. The vector does not inject the trypanosomes when it jabs because they do not enter its salivary glands as in the tsetse. Instead they travel along the gut of the reduviid and are passed out with the faeces on the host's skin. As a result of the irritation caused by the very painful jab the host scratches the wound, and so brings the trypanosomes into contact with his blood. This self infection is particularly efficacious because the bugs usually attack sleeping people at night so that reflex scratching occurs. If the human hosts should wake it is unlikely that they will refrain from scratching, even if taught the danger, because the bugs generally bite very young children. Chagas' desease may be mild, but if the cardiac muscle is affected it can lead to early death. Alternatively a combination of anaemia and damage to the heart may produce chronic weakness and eventually death. An obvious control is to render houses more suitable for destruction of the reduviids by insecticides, but in developing countries where the disease is endemic it can spread from the countryside to the growing shanty towns in which housing is of so poor a standard that effective spraying is difficult; another example of an economic problem lying at the root of a medical one. The World Health Organization in 1960 estimated that 7 000 000 people were affected by Chagas' disease.

It is difficult to express the economic burden of trypanosomiasis. In human terms the loss in incalculable. The debilitating effect on the quality of life and the discouragement of the economic aspirations of a population which lives in a state of chronic and sometimes acute ill health are probably difficult for those who live in the developed countries to grasp fully. It is not possible to assess in financial terms the cost of control measures as compared with the benefits which they confer because figures for both sides of the equation are lacking in almost every country.

In 1962 the FAO estimated that a potential capital value of US $5 000 000 000 was lost through permanent infestation by tsetse. The implication is that eradication would permit the value to be realized, but such an assessment makes all sorts of political and economic assumptions. In practice most African countries take the view that the losses caused by the fly justify any attempt at control.

The mosquito-borne diseases

Mosquitoes, unlike the tsetse, have an almost world-wide distribution and, although today their economic importance is limited to tropical and sub-tropical countries, malaria used to be a common disease in northern Europe and Asia. Its virtual eradication from these areas in the course of the last hundred years has been achieved partly by deliberate control but largely as a by-product of improved agriculture and swamp clearance which were not originally intended as means for controlling malaria.

Many of the mosquito-borne diseases stem from natural reservoirs amongst both primate and non primate alternative hosts. Eradication is rendered even more difficult by the large number of mosquito species and their very varied ecology, which means that the control measures have to be accurately aimed at the particular species. The following table brings out some of these points.

Disease	Parasite	Vector	Vector's breeding habits	Alternative hosts
Malaria	Protozoan *Plasmodium*	*Anopheles* spp. especially *A. gambiae* and *A. stephensi*	Domestic and ground water generally	None
Filariasis	Nematodes *Wuchereria bancrofti*	In rural areas *Anopheles* spp.	Domestic and ground water generally	None
		In urban areas *Culex pipiens fatigans*	Especially domestic	None
	Brugia malayi	*Anopheles* spp. and *Mansonia* spp.	Ground water generally	Monkeys, wild & domestic cats
Yellow Fever *Jungle form*	Virus	*Aedes* spp.	Forest	Monkeys
Urban form	Virus	*Aedes aegypti*	Especially domestic, also forest.	Monkeys
Dengue	Virus	*Aedes aegypti*	as above	Monkeys
West Nile	Virus	*Culex*		Birds
Chikungunya	Virus	*Aedes aegypti*	Domestic	Probably none
Onyongnyong	Virus	*Anopheles gambiae* and *A. funestus*	Domestic and ground water generally	None
Encephalitis St Louis	Virus	*Culex*	Domestic	Birds
California	Virus	*Aedes* spp.	Ground pools and containers	Rodents
Western equine	Virus	*Culex tarsalis*	as above	Birds
Japanese B	Virus	*Culex tritaenio-rhynchus*	as above	Pigs and some wading birds

The importance of the mosquito cannot be grasped without some knowledge of the mosquito-borne diseases. Malaria is the most widespread, occurring in virtually all tropical, sub-tropical and warm temperate countries. Where it does not exist in these regions the danger of its introduction is always present. The World Health Organization estimated in 1971 that eradication programmes were protecting 619 000 000 people, substantial anti-malarial operations were giving a further 195 000 000 some degree of protection and 272 000 000 lived in unprotected malarious areas. Much has therefore already been done, but the struggle never ends. After the initial great success of synthetic insecticides workers began to think in terms of eradicating the disease rather than merely controlling it. Unfortunately the cost of eradication is very great not only in terms of swamp clearance and spraying in difficult territory but also on account of the back-up services needed in an all-out eradication programme, such as the provision of drugs and medical personnel and the education of large populations in anti-malaria precautions. These costs cannot be borne by the developing countries where the need is greatest, and consequently in many places the concept of eradication – which is a theoretical possibility – has, for the time being, given way to the less ambitious, but still enormous, task of control. We do not propose to describe the life history of the various species of malarial parasite but it is worth mentioning some effects of the disease. Malaria *can* be relatively mild, producing symptoms not unlike those of influenza – high temperature, shivering and sweating – but the form caused by *Plasmodium falciparum* can lead to unconsciousness or very severe vomiting and even to the formation of blood clots in the brain. In the malarious areas the local population may possess some immunity through having been exposed to the disease for many generations so that it suffers less than do immigrants. Even so, the relative immunity may be only at the cost of a general lowering of physical condition as in the case of African negroes amongst whom a high proportion of individuals are heterozygous for sickle-cell haemoglobin. The sickle gene is sub-lethal in the homozygous condition because it leads to severe anaemia and usually to death before the age of reproduction, and would be expected to disappear from the population. It survives, however, because in heterozygous individuals it confers some immunity against the very dangerous form of malaria caused by *P. falciparum*, whereas normal individuals have none. Heterozygotes do suffer from anaemia, though much less than homozygotes, so the immunity is achieved only at a cost. Anaemia is a feature of chronic malaria because the body's reaction to the release of merozoites into the blood, and their subsequent invasion of erythrocytes, is to produce an abundant supply of phagocytes in response. The phagocytes then engulf the affected erythrocytes. The anaemia might not, by itself, be excessively debilitating in the long run; indeed Europeans who are infected with the milder species of malarial parasite usually recover and are fit for normal work, but the parasite's effect on people who are already undernourished and affected by other debilitating tropical parasites is very serious. In turn it lowers resistance to other diseases and reduces the population's capacity and inclination for work, so that malaria control is a first essential for the material growth of any affected country.

Filariasis is a widespread nematode disease in Southern Europe, Africa, Asia, Australia, Polynesia and South America. The more important parasite is *Wuchereria bancrofti* whose only vertebrate host is man, but *Brugia malayi*, which is confined to Asia, exists in many vertebrate hosts.

W. bancrofti occurs mainly along the coastline of the countries in its area but *B. malayi* may occur far inland. The adults live in the human lymphatic system where the females give rise to larvae which hatch *in utero*. These larvae are known as microfilariae. They escape from the parent and migrate to the blood where their development cannot proceed unless they are sucked by a mosquito. From the mosquito's gut they migrate to the flight muscles, and pass through two further larval stages. The final stage is infective if returned to the blood of a human host. It seems that the larvae are not injected into the human host with the mosquito's saliva but escape by penetrating through the thin cuticle of the labium and, travelling down the proboscis externally, enter the human host probably through the hole pierced by the mosquito. They travel to the lymphatic system and develop into adult worms about one centimetre in length which live for up to five years in the host. They may cause lesions and inflammation in the lymphatic system which the patient feels as pain in the affected region and a general aching sensation. Later the blocking of the lymph vessels and growth of connective tissue stimulated by the presence of the parasite may lead to the extreme swelling of legs and genital organs known as elephantiasis. Whilst the extreme manifestations are rare, such distress is caused by the lengthy progress of filariasis that it counts as a major disease.

Two biological forms of *W. bancrofti* exist, although the adults are indistinguishable, and they are associated with different species of mosquito. In one form the microfilariae are present in the peripheral circulation only at night, in the other during the day. The former is the more widespread and is transmitted by nocturnally-biting species of *Anopheles* and *Culex pipiens fatigans*, whereas the diurnally periodic form, which is confined to Polynesia, is transmitted by day-biting species of *Aedes*.

The control of the mosquitoes follows the general principles which are described below with the additional problem of *Mansonia*, one of the vectors of *B. malayi*. The larvae of *Mansonia* do not rise to the surface to breathe but thrust their spiracles into water plants and obtain oxygen through the plants' intercellular spaces, which also renders them safe from attack by insecticides spread on the surface of the water. The use of herbicides has proved an effective control in Ceylon.

Yellow fever is the best known of the arbovirus diseases. An arbovirus is a virus of vertebrates which is transmitted by arthropods. There are about three hundred of them, only a third of which cause disease in man. With very few exceptions, however, they exist outside man in other vertebrates, especially primates, rodents and birds, which have acquired a tolerance for them and provide a reservoir of infection. The principal vectors, and the only ones which we shall consider, are mosquitoes, but mites and ticks transmit some of the viruses.

The arbovirus diseases cause epidemics in all parts of the world, especially in the tropics. Most are not fatal: they cause severe fever and temporary disabling (dengue, West Nile, chikungunya and onyongnyong for example) but leave no after-effects. Some forms of encephalitis and, of course, yellow fever have a high death rate. In its classical form yellow fever is a disease of large human concentrations in tropical countries, where it is transmitted from man to man by *Aedes aegypti* whose choice of breeding places makes it a particularly dangerous urban pest. In Brazil in 1932, the disease was found to occur in the jungle, where it is transmitted by other species of *Aedes* which suck blood from monkeys, opossums, rodents and other forest mammals. The virus of jungle yellow fever is the same as that of the urban form and, since it can be transmitted to man by the forest mosquitoes which normally feed on animals, provides a reservoir from which urban populations can be re-infected. This is particularly serious at a time when the jungle is being opened up to exploration and there is much movement of people between jungle and cities.

Mosquito control

Effective control measures always stem from a true appreciation of the insects' ecology, and in the case of mosquitoes it is made more difficult by virtue of the varied habits of the pest species.

Attacking the adult insect is expensive but often necessary. The ideal control method is to break the life cycle by poisoning the larvae or, in the long term, by destroying their habitats. On a small scale, and in relatively developed countries, such as in southern Europe and in Mediterranean islands, it has been possible to eradicate the mosquito by draining swamps and then suitably protecting reservoirs of drinking water. On a large scale in tropical countries it is almost impossible. Mosquitoes are much less particular about where they will breed than are tsetse flies: almost any body of still or running water will serve for some species of danger-ous mosquito. In areas of very heavy rainfall, which will inevitably be thickly covered in vegetation, innumerable potential breeding sites will be created by every torrent of rain filling not only permanent hollows in the ground or on trees but also the impressions made by the hooves of cattle and game animals. Since under tropical or sub-tropical conditions no more than six days are needed for *Anopheles gambiae* to develop from newly deposited egg to adult it is evident that to try and spray a significant proportion of temporary habitats in time to kill larvae is a hopeless task. It is therefore necessary to back up measures against the larvae with direct action against the adults.

Control of mosquitoes which breed near human habitation   The domestic mos-quitoes, in both rural and urban areas lend themselves most readily to anti-larval measures which come almost under the description of hygiene.

The principal species are *Anopheles gambiae* (which is not in the least confined to domestic habitats), *Anopheles stephensi*, which is often domestic and *Aedes aegypti* and *Culex pipiens fatigans* which are primarily domestic. The immediate presence of man offers abundant habitats in the form of water butts, surface and underground cisterns, wells, cesspits and septic tanks, sagging sections of roof-gutters and any old bowls and cans which are left lying about. Apart from the obvious, though not easily enforced, measures of communal tidiness much can be done to restrict these habitats by covering cisterns and wells with tightly fitting lids and also by blocking up hollows in trees since many of the minor vector species habitually breed there. Cesspits and open latrines are very difficult to cover adequately. The complete eradication of *Culex pipiens fatigans* must probably await the introduction of proper sanitation in urban areas – not that urbanization is necessarily the answer to the control of all species since industrial waste, especially if it encourages the growth of vegetation, may provide habitats for anophelines. A layer of oil spread over the surface of drinking water in large containers is effective until it becomes broken by the wind. In large containers fish can be used as a form of biological control, with the added advantage of providing a source of protein for human consumption.

Urbanization in developing countries, because it is usually indiscriminate and so rapid that the authorities cannot properly contain it, creates problems of its own. Haphazard building operations produce breeding places in the form of trenches and borrow-pits; large numbers of people living roughly scatter tin cans and old motor tyres all of which need only a sudden shower to fill them with enough water for the domestic species to multiply.

Finally irrigation channels close to small rural populations present a problem which calls for the use of insecticides in the same way as do other large bodies of static or slowly moving ground water.

A simple but effective means of reducing mosquito populations near human habitation is to remove ground vegetation from the vicinity. Most of the dangerous mosquitoes suck blood after dark (*Aedes aegypti* is exceptional in being diurnal) and shelter in the vegetation during the day. An obvious disadvantage of this control measure is that in hot countries the cutting or burning of vegetation has to be repeated frequently, and a small untreated patch will harbour enough adults to restore a dangerous population.

Whilst the domestic species can theoretically be dealt with by sanitation and relatively simple precautions, such measures are not sufficiently available in rural areas and in urban ones where administrative control cannot cope with the scale of the problem. Insecticides directed against the adults are essential. They are applied chiefly inside buildings, the walls being sprayed with residual insecticides especially DDT and Gammexane. No blanket control exists however, partly because of the resistance to particular insecticides which species may develop and partly because of the difficulty of deciding on the irritant action of many insecticides. The battle with the domestic mosquito is best conducted as a varied campaign employing tactics against both the larvae and adults, using different insecticides according to the needs of the moment.

The success and endurance of the domestic species stems partly from the fact that they are extremely good travellers. *Anopheles gambiae* spread from West Africa to Brazil before the Second World War and caused much damage: its eradication in Brazil in 1940 is one of the great successes in malaria control. *Aedes aegypti* travels well by all means of transport, and air transport presents a threat to tropical countries in which yellow fever does not occur. *Ae. aegypti* is said even to breed on board ship.

Control of mosquitoes over a large area   The eradication of mosquitoes from the proximity of man is rendered yet more difficult by the fact that they have considerable powers of dispersal. Species vary very much in their power of flight but, with the help of air currents, most species can travel many miles from their emergence site. Consequently even good standards of hygiene near human habitation cannot prevent adult mosquitoes arriving from the bush. The best long term measure is therefore the destruction of the insects or, better still, of their breeding sites, over a large area. In large underdeveloped countries the cost of swamp drainage on a large scale is prohibitive, so once more insecticides are brought to bear. The classic method is to oil the surface of swamps and ponds. It used to be thought that the oil's effect of lowering the surface tension of the water made it impossible for the larvae and pupae to cling to the surface when coming up for air, but we now know that the oil acts as a poison − it is in fact an insecticide. It has, however, many disadvantages. The film may be disrupted by wind, especially on a large body of water, and near the margins of a lake where many anopheline species breed the fringing vegetation interferes with the spreading of the oil to form a satisfactory film. In addition it is not easy to spread oil satisfactorily from the air on to a large lake or swamp.

Insecticides such as DDT and Gammexane can easily be sprayed from the air and are effective because they spread throughout the body of the water, but again, since almost any temporary hollow will provide a breeding place attempts have been made to spray the bush with insecticide on a large scale. That is no longer considered a suitable technique on account of the random effect of the insecticides: control measures have become more sophisticated and include genetic control.

The non-domestic species of mosquito, too, may benefit from the beginnings of economic development. Deforestation can cause a sudden increase in population by giving ground pools access to sunlight, and the construction of dams creates perfect habitats. So does irrigation, especially in rice fields: Japanese encephalitis and malaria have been spread in this manner. Irrigation, leading to a rise in relative humidity can not only create more breeding places but, by increasing the longevity of the mosquitoes, enables them to spread more infections. It can also favour the more dangerous species at the expense of the less dangerous. It is ironical that projects which carry great potential benefits should be haunted by almost equal perils. The lesson to be learnt is that no development should be allowed to proceed indiscriminately but that the predictable ill effects should be taken into consideration, and adequate counter measures be made available, from the beginning.

The flea-borne diseases, lice-borne diseases and bed bugs

The serious medical importance of fleas (pages 51 and 98) has declined in developed countries owing to domestic hygiene, including rat eradication, and not least to the use of the vacuum cleaner which disturbs the environment in which the insects' eggs develop. In those countries the human flea, *Pulex irritans*, has become scarce and man is more likely to be bitten by the parasites of his domestic dogs and cats: the bites of these fleas are unlikely to transmit disease, although they may be very painful to susceptible individuals, but scratching may produce infection. In general the various species of flea have one or more preferred hosts but many will bite man as well. The most serious pest is *Xenopsylla cheopis*, the Oriental rat flea, which transmits *Bacillus pestis*, the causative organism of bubonic plague, from rat to rat and from rat to man. It is essentially a rat parasite which transfers its attention to man when many rats have been killed by the bacterium. The bacterium multiplies in the flea's alimentary canal, clogging it so that blood sucking is rendered impossible. In its attempts at sucking the flea regurgitates bacteria into the man's blood. The human flea can transmit plague from rat to rat and from man to man so it can be seen that danger of epidemic exists in countries where hygiene is of a low standard. Should a natural disaster such as an earthquake cause not only the collapse of normal sanitary services but also a crowding together of refugees under bad conditions, the presence of a few affected individuals, who might normally have been contained, may suffice to spark off an epidemic. The flea, then, is a potential danger. Not only *Xenopsylla cheopis* but the European rat flea, *Nosopsyllus fasciatus*, and the cat and dog fleas *Ctenocephalides felis* and *Ct. canis* (Figure 2.15) respectively, are cosmopolitan. In Britain the cat flea, from domestic pets, provides the vast majority of infestations. All transmit murine or endemic typhus from rat to rat and from rat to man. Murine typhus, caused by *Rickettsia typhi*, is still a considerable menace in Asia and parts of eastern Europe. The association between the fleas and the *Rickettsia* is probably of long standing for the fleas suffer no ill effect.

All fleas can be controlled by simple hygienic precautions. The key to controlling fleas lies in denying them suitable breeding conditions which can be done by removing dirt, in which the larvae find their food, especially the partially digested blood in the faeces of the adults, and by shaking out rugs and blankets in which eggs may be laid, and where the right microclimate of temperature and humidity exists. Fleas' eggs are not stuck to the substratum and readily fall off it on shaking. In the case of serious infestation houses can be fumigated against the human flea while cats and dogs can be dusted with finely powdered pyrethrum or rotenone which are not harmful to mammals. Perhaps the most important measure of all, against plague and murine typhus, is rat control.

The sucking lice, Order Siphunculata (page 46) may also transmit rickettsial and other diseases, but not in north western Europe. Both nymphs and adults cause painful bites, suck blood and, when they are present in large numbers, cause considerable distress through loss of sleep. A badly infested person is almost certain to scratch and acquire secondary infection. The common species is *Pediculus humanus* which exists in two forms the head louse, *P.h. capitis*, and the body louse, *P.h. corporis*, which are best described as sub-species because their ecology normally keeps them apart, although they can be crossed readily in captivity. Whereas the head louse feeds on the scalp and lays its eggs, 'nits', on the hair the body louse feeds on other parts of the body: it sometimes lays its eggs on body hairs but more commonly in the clothing, especially along seams or folds. The body louse is slightly the larger but morphological differences are slight. In all probability the physical proximity of the two forms on the parasitized individual provides enough possibility of cross-mating to prevent the forms from becoming biological species.

The other human louse is *Phthirus pubis*, the crab louse (Figure 2.7), so called because of its massive claws with which it clings to the hair, mostly in the pubic region. None of the lice can survive for long away from a host: unlike the fleas they cannot remain without feeding and are highly susceptible to temperature changes. The body lice are the most independent, being able to survive in the microclimate of clothing which has been removed for the night. Not even they can develop except at temperatures very close to that of the human body.

Pediculus is the vector of epidemic or exanthematous typhus, trench fever and European relapsing fever: *Phthirus* is not known to transmit any disease though scratching by the infested person may permit bacteria to enter the bites. In all probability the pathogens associated with *Pediculus* are transmitted less often through the direct bite of the lice than by their excreta or dead bodies being rubbed into the bites.

Epidemic typhus is caused by *Rickettsia prowazeki* which lives intracellularly in the gut of the louse and is fatal to it. The parasitic relationship, unlike that between the fleas and *R. typhi*, is of fairly recent origin. Epidemic typhus is still the cause of serious epidemics in the East. Trench fever is caused by *R. quintans* which multiplies extracellularly in the lumen of the louse's gut. The disease, which was serious during the First World War, vanished from Europe immediately after it. Outbreaks of epidemic relapsing fever still occur in Europe. It is caused by a bacterium, *Spirochaeta recurrentis* which is not infective until it has been through the body of the louse. This infection is never caused by biting but exclusively by inoculation, when the lice are crushed and the spirochaetes enter the human body through breaks in the skin. Since each louse can infect only one man the disease cannot assume epidemic proportions unless people are crowded together in insalubrious conditions. In hot countries the symptoms of relapsing fever are probably often confused with those of malaria.

In Britain head lice are still a problem in spite of a high level of general hygiene. Fashion is partly responsible: hair which is left uncombed either in the interests of a particular style or through negligence is vulnerable. Since people are often ashamed of admitting to being lousy they put off reporting the infestation until it is well established. Head louse infestation occurs mainly among children and young people, but body lice are more likely to infest the elderly and infirm especially if they are poor. The correlation between infestation and social conditions and hygiene is obvious.

An infestation can develop rapidly owing to the high reproductive rate of all lice. Transmission can occur whenever people are in contact; the head louse is spread from one school child to another during games, the body louse in common lodging houses or in camps for displaced persons, the crab louse usually through sexual intercourse. Control is essentially a matter of prevention by ordinary hygiene, but if an infestation occurs it can be dealt with quickly by simple treatment with insecticides and physical measures. Head louse populations can be killed rapidly by carefully rubbing in Lethane hair oil, after which the hair should be combed regularly in order to remove the tightly cemented nits. Body lice can be killed by dusting the bedclothes and underclothes, especially the seams, with a persistent insecticide such as BHC. Really effective laundering too can kill all stages of the life history. The great problem with any louse infestation is to prevent re-infestation of the de-loused individuals. For this reason when large infestations are being dealt with, such as in wartime or in disaster areas, de-lousing is a major operation which involves central-ized laundering, isolation and a programme of education in hygiene.

It is convenient at this point to mention one other blood-sucking pest which is not, as far as we know, the vector of any disease but a considerable nuisance. The bed bug, *Cimex* (Hemiptera: Cimicidae, Figure 2.9) is cosmopolitan. It feeds on alternate nights. It does not live on its host but in cracks in furniture where it can survive for as much as a year without feeding: the removal of timber from an in-fested house is one means of transmission. Its jab is painful and causes loss of sleep. Control by means of residual insecticides is easy provided that social conditions permit their effective use.

Cornwell draws attention to a surprising pattern of flea and bed bug infestation in Britain.[6] Before the Second World War both insects were associated with con-ditions of low hygiene in slum property in London and other big industrial cities. A survey made between 1967 and 1973 revealed that outside London and Mersey-side, which retained high infestations, the holiday areas of Wales and the West Country were the most heavily infested. The unlikely distribution may be due to the evacuation of large numbers of people from the major cities during the war, which brought the urban pests to areas of low population. In Britain today fleas, though still minor pests, are increasing in number. They are no longer necessarily a sign of poverty but have benefited from the introduction of elaborate central heating installations in office blocks, large stores and even hospitals, whose base-ments and hot-air ducting often contain large populations of neglected cats from which the cat flea can spread to man.

Cockroaches

We must consider one further insect which can be a disease carrier but whose status as a pest derives rather from the disgust which it evokes in many people — the cockroach. Only a few species are associated with man, the vast majority living permanently out of doors, but owing to their high reproductive capacity, extreme adaptability and omnivorous feeding they readily become pests. Man provides them with shelter and heat in his buildings, where they also find abundant food. Insti-tutions with extensive underground passages and heating systems provide all the requirements; catering establishments, food factories, laundries and ironically, hospitals, as well as domestic dwellings are ideal environments. So are ships, and the important pest species have become cosmopolitan.

The causative organisms of several diseases have been identified in the gut and faeces, and on the cuticle, of most of the pest species, but there is no direct evidence of the cockroaches having acted as vectors. All the same their habits render them suspect; for example if they breed near the privies or waste-disposal areas of cater-ing establishments they may contaminate food by regurgitation, and in hospitals they have been known to run over patients' beds at night. The pathogens which may be carried include the causative organisms of food poisoning, typhoid, dysentery and gastroenteritis. Apart from the possible health hazard cockroaches are a source of loss in stored foods in catering establishments and warehouses, not only because of what they eat but because of their soiling action. Consequently energetic efforts should be made to control them, in the first place by good hygiene especially in privies and rubbish heaps, and by insecticides. Chlordane has been widely used, and in 1953 resistance to it was detected in *Blattella germanica* in the USA. The resistance was linked with resistance to other chlorinated hydrocarbons. In Britain the same insect has developed resistance to dieldrin. An alternative is the carbamate insecticide propoxur (or aprocarb) which is persistent and also stimulates the insects into activity so that the operators are able to see where more should be applied, a particularly useful property when dealing with cockroaches which remain concealed in large aggregations for most of the day. The retiring nature of cockroaches also makes poisoned baits a useful weapon in places where sprays are inappropriate, for example where food might be contaminated or in zoos where animals might be poisoned. For this purpose chlordecone is often used, and laid so as to be inaccessible to man and domestic animals. Another modern insecticide is the carbamate bendiocarb, marketed as FICAM W (Figure 6.2) which can be applied as a water spray to the places frequented by cockroaches, fleas and many other pests. It is said to be harmless to man and domestic animals at the prescribed dosage but the manufacturer's instructions should be scrupulously adhered to, as in the case of all insecticides.

Pests of Agriculture
Termites

Most of the insect pests of growing crops wreak their damage either directly, or indirectly by acting as vectors for micro-organisms, on the plant itself. Few have a major effect on the soil except by their action as scavengers in breaking down particles of dead vegetable matter in the early stages of humification. Termites are an exception and, in spite of being pests of several species of tropical crops, contribute to the improvement of soils in tropical countries. In Africa much damage is done to the soil by destruction of forest, by shifting agriculture in which an area is worked to exhaustion and then abandoned, and by over-grazing. Mound-building termites are a stage in the natural regeneration of forest. Although the mounds are bare of vegetation while termites are active in their outer layers, very large mounds have a thick wall of soil whose function is to insulate the colony and from which the insects are absent. Grass grows over such mounds, and also over any which have been abandoned by their colonies. The grass cover stops erosion of the mounds and, in time, shrubs and even tall trees come to grow on them producing a peculiar landscape in which trees appear to be growing on pedestals. When the mounds are sufficiently close the shade cover produced by the trees is continuous. Under the protection of this canopy the ground is protected from further erosion, and woodland regenerates. In the intervening period the trees which grow on the mounds can survive the grass fires which are a feature of tropical Africa. Termites also improve the soil by the aerating effects of the tunnels which subterranean species excavate, and by bringing material from lower levels to the surface, so performing a function similar to that of earthworms in temperate climates.

The beneficial action of the mound-builders is not, however, matched by other termites. There are many species of harvesters which make subterranean nests from which they forage for grass. By consuming large quantities they reduce the amount available for the sustenance of farm animals: too much grass is stripped from the ground and erosion follows, probably hastened by the action of hooves cutting up the unprotected soil. This in turn creates bare patches, which makes it easier for the founders of new colonies to penetrate the soil after the swarming flight.

Some of the grass-eating termites build small mounds which makes their control relatively easy, though laborious: the mounds are first broken open and then treated with a dieldrin suspension in water. The most serious pest, however, is the true harvester, *Hodotermes mossambicus*, whose range extends into most of the arid lands of central and southern Africa. Its subterranean nests cannot be attacked directly but the insects can be destroyed by spreading a poisoned bait, in the form of hay or wheat chaff soaked in sodium fluorosilicate, over the infested ground.

Termites are probably not primary pests of agriculture except in the case of the rubber tree. A primary pest is one which attacks intact plants: termites customarily attack those which have suffered some setback such as weakening through drought, fungus attack or pruning which has left imperfectly callused wounds. Even normal agricultural operations such as weeding or hoeing, which result in slight damage to some part of the root system, produce a route through which wood-eating termites can penetrate. The roots of rubber trees may be so weakened by the galleries which they make that the trees fall over without warning. Termites, as secondary pests, attack most tropical crops including cocoa, tea, sugar cane and cereals. Their control is made difficult because they do not need specific food plants: since they will feed on most woody tissues they are always available to reinfest any tropical plantation from which they have been cleared, which can be done by using chlorinated hydrocarbons properly applied. Good agricultural practice such as the removal of stumps of affected trees and care in hoeing will help to reduce the danger of infestation.

Locusts

Among the most ancient and potentially the most widespread serious pests of standing crops are locusts. Their action has largely been contained by energetic means of control, which are expensive to maintain but essential in view of the far greater cost of serious outbreaks. The necessary knowledge now exists, and only material considerations stand in the way of almost complete control. The need for control is accentuated by the fact that the areas in which locusts are most likely to cause damage include the countries of the Third World, which can least afford it.

Locusts are polymorphic shorthorn grasshoppers (Orthoptera: Acrididae). The polymorphism includes not only profound morphological differences but also even more remarkable differences in behaviour. In 1921 Uvarov, working in Russia, showed that the migratory locust *Locusta migratoria,* existed in the extreme forms known as *phases.* The term phase is unfortunate since it suggests that the individual will change from one phase into another: it may, but may equally spend the whole of its nymphal and adult life in one phase. Intermediate forms exist between the phases, so that a continuous series can be demonstrated if pinned specimens are placed alongside each other, but at the extremes the differences are so great that the individuals were formerly thought to be of different species. Not only the adults but also the hoppers (nymphs) of the phases differ.

The following table compares some morphological features of members of the solitary and gregarious phases of *Locusta migratoria.*

		Solitary	*Gregarious*
HOPPERS	*Colour*	Often uniform	Black pattern on orange background
	Length of femora	Shorter	Longer
ADULTS	*Colour*	A darker pattern than in the gregarious phase	Colour may vary during life
	Total size	Larger	Smaller
	Length of femora	Longer	Shorter
	Length of fore-wing/ length of femur	Less	Greater
	Shape of pronotum (in lateral view)		

The important difference between the phases lies in their behaviour, which may be either solitary or gregarious. *Locusta migratoria* ph. *danica,* the solitary phase, is widespread. The term solitary is misleading. Where conditions are suitable *danica* can exist in large numbers, and can be a minor pest in the same way as some grass-hopper species. Members of the solitary phase do not react to each other's presence in any remarkable way. They just carry on with the business of eating. Members of the gregarious phase, *migratoria,* however, influence each other's movements both in the hopper and adult stages: the movement of one individual stimulates move-ments in its neighbours leading, in the case of the hoppers, to the formation of wandering bands and, in the winged adults, to migrating swarms. What happens is that under particularly suitable breeding conditions of locality, temperature and freedom from natural enemies, the population builds up within a certain area. The process may require more than one season. The emergence of a large number of hoppers in close proximity releases their gregarious behaviour. From the beginning the hoppers tend to keep together and to imitate each other's movements. This results in the formation of small groups which move in unison. Fortuitously two bands converge, and then act as a single band. The process continues and eventually a large band is formed. During the day it feeds and at night its members climb on the vegetation and rest until the heat of the sun on the following day permits the resumption of their activity. When the band has become very large it begins to march, the individuals at first hopping in different directions. Gradually a common direction is evolved and once the march has begun it has to continue in the set direction because of the mutual stimulation of the members. The advance is usually on a broad front, unless the surface of the ground or its vegetation prevents it, and the pressure of the hoppers in the rear makes it impossible for those in front to turn back; movement stimulates movement, always forward. A large wandering band will gather up others as it travels, unsurmountable obstacles are circumvented and water is no barrier since the hoppers can swim. The band will halt either when the heat is too great, when the hoppers shelter under shade, or in the evening when they climb up plants and feed.

In the course of their wandering the hoppers moult, eventually becoming winged adults. Marching is then replaced by swarming. At first the flights are brief, and circular, the individuals on the ground again matching their more active neighbours' movements and taking off. Eventually the whole swarm is in flight, and at this stage may stimulate grounded swarms to fly and join it so that a vast swarm is produced. Flight then ceases to be circular and assumes a definite direction which may be maintained for as much as seventy hours, the locusts flying by night as well as by day. When either adverse external conditions or the draining of internal energy supplies compels the migrating swarm to land it returns to its pre-migrating pattern of circular flights until oviposition begins.

Now, although the solitary phase is very widespread the number of areas that are suitable as breeding places for the gregarious phase is limited and can be hundreds of kilometres away from the areas in which the migrating swarms produce their plagues. The formation of the gregarious phase is associated with breeding in regions of vast reed-swamps (especially of *Phragmites communis*) with enough exposed raised areas for oviposition and a high mean temperature, conditions which prevail in Turkistan (Figure 6.5), the breeding place of *migratoria*. These breeding places are known as *outbreak areas*.

Several sub-species of *Locusta migratoria* exist, each of which has its solitary and gregarious phase. In the case of *Locusta migratoria migratoria* the solitary phase is *danica* and the gregarious phase is know as *migratoria*: it is a little unfortunate that the phase name should be identical with the specific name. *L. m. migratoria* is the Asiatic migratory locust whose range includes mid Asia, the Caucasus, the southern Ukraine and Romania. The principal other sub-species is *L. m. migratorioides*, in tropical Africa. For a long time it was not realized that the migratory locust was polytypic and the phase *migratorioides* was used to describe the gregarious phase in tropical Africa of what was then thought to be the monotypic species *L. migratoria*. Other sub-species include *L.m. gallica* in south western France and *L. m. capito* in Madagascar.

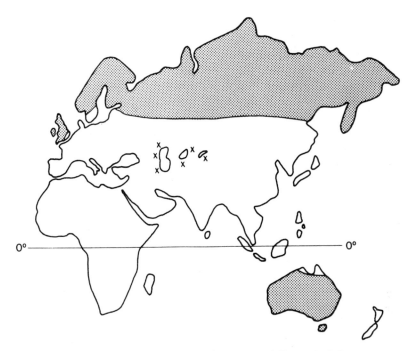

Figure 6.5 *Distribution of the migratory locust* (after Uvarov) The unshaded area represents the territory of the various sub-species of *Locusta migratoria.* The crosses indicate the breeding areas of the gregarious phase of *L.m.migratoria.*

Locusta migratoria is one of the best studied species but it is not the greatest pest, probably because the hoppers feed mainly on plants of the Family Graminae (it can be a serious pest on rice) and the adults eat relatively little although they may do serious damage to many plants including trees whose leaves they nibble, in order to satisfy their water requirements, causing them to fall off. Most locusts, however, when swarming will eat any available fresh plant material.

Among the most serious pests in the Old World are the desert locust, *Schistocerca gregaria,* the brown locust, *Locustana pardalina,* and the red locust, *Nomadacris septemfasciata. Schistocerca paranensis* is widespread in South and Central America. The control of locusts depends in the first place on research to determine the areas in which the gregarious phase may develop, then to determine the conditions which govern the emergence of swarms so that their periodicity may be predicted. These factors vary from species to species and even intraspecifically from country to country. Even if firm ecological evidence is available as to general locality and conditions it may be very difficult actually to locate individual swarms at an early stage, especially in extensive or inaccessible country.

Once bands of hoppers have been located, however, modern methods can quickly be brought to bear on them. The use of environmentally undesirable insecticides, spread from the air, is justifiable in view of the potential danger of a locust plague especially when the early stages of a migration take place in uninhabited country as is the case with the desert locust.

The basic knowledge now exists for preventing major outbreaks of the
African migratory locust and the red locust because, as in the case of the Asiatic
migratory locust, there are relatively small well defined outbreak areas in which
the solitary form can always be found — although the invasion area, should a plague
break out, may cover between half and two thirds of Africa. The outbreak areas
may be inaccessible but at least they are identifiable, and control rests largely on
sound technology, administration and international co-operation. Most of the
pest species, however, are not so amenable: they will not let themselves be hit
in restricted outbreak areas. The chief example is the desert locust, on which
most modern research is done. We see from Figure 6.6. that its invasion area
surrounds an enormous *recession area* from which the solitary form is never
absent. The right conditions for production of the gregarious phase may occur
anywhere in the invasion area and under adverse conditions the species survives in
the recession area where fresh swarms may form under suitable conditions. The
problem of policing these vast areas is so intractable that the desert locust is
still the most serious agricultural pest in the Old World on account not only of
the damage which it does when swarms occur but also of the strain on resources
which prevention entails. As always the answer to the problem lies first with
ecology. Although the locust may occur anywhere within the invasion and
recession areas its movements are not random. Not every locality within it is always
suitable for breeding. As amateur breeders of *Schistocerca* will have discovered,
in the laboratory, humidity is critical to the development of the eggs and is not

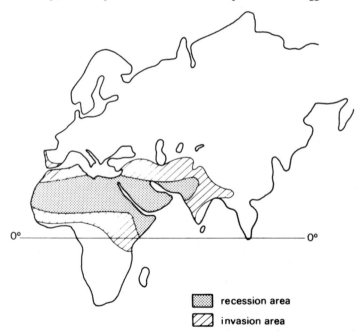

Figure 6.6 *Distribution of the desert locust* (based on material supplied by the Centre for
Overseas Pest Research)

easy to regulate. In nature the swarms in the invasion areas migrate, finding areas in which the humidity is suitable and breeding there. In that way swarming can continue for many years, but not in the same place. Left to themselves the swarming populations would sooner or later come to an end through the action of natural enemies, but agriculture cannot wait for that. If the locust control organizations can predict the path of the migrations they can strike early at the swarms, and at this point meteorology comes to the help of control. When locusts begin to fly they take off into the wind but once airborne *Schistocerca* flies with the wind. In fact they may sometimes fly at any angle to it, but since the speed of prevailing winds is greater than that of the insects the net result is downwind movement of the swarm often at a speed rather less than that of the wind. In that way the desert locust can easily cover one hundred kilometres in a day. Now, the air streams in the area which the locusts inhabit converge, and where they meet rain falls, the arid region becomes temporarily moist and a sudden growth of vegetation occurs. The result of the locusts' way of travelling is therefore to bring them to regions where they will find food which enables them to continue their migration. While the swarms are wandering in the desert they do no harm, but their migration routes inevitably take them into cultivated areas so that in a swarming year there is always the danger of a plague. Records of locust populations, or a least the best estimates, are sent by all the countries which observe them to the Centre for Overseas Pest Research, in London, where a monthly analysis of them, together with meteorological information, is published. On the basis of the information control teams in countries that are likely to be affected can act appropriately. The chief difficulty is to obtain reliable information.

The wandering bands of hoppers are not easily spotted from the air, but infrared techniques may prove to be useful and radar is used for following the movement of swarms up to a distance of eighty kilometres. In view of the extent and difficulty of the area, spotting the swarms remains the greatest single control problem.

Nowadays insecticides are virtually the sole weapons although, before the advent of chlorinated hydrocarbons, trenches and poisoned baits were widely used against hoppers. Dieldrin and Lindane are standard insecticides today. Their environmental danger is much reduced owing to the method of application which consists of spraying a concentrated oil solution in very fine droplets, either from the ground or from the air, so as to give an extremely uniform coverage. In this way the quantity of insecticide applied to a given area is kept low, which is economically as well as environmentally desirable. In any case the application of residual insecticides to constantly changing locust areas cannot have the same long term effects as would their repeated use on field crops in one area.

For anti-locust work alternative methods, such as biological or genetic control are even less likely to be of any use in the foreseeable future than they are in the case of tsetse and mosquitoes.

The Director of the Centre for Overseas Pest Research, Dr P.T. Haskell describes a serious difficulty for the future of locust control, the 'problem of success'.[7] Now that the worst effects of the pest are fairly successfuly overcome some governments which are looking for economies are cutting down on the allocation of funds to research. The very nature of the anti-locust problem, with long periods in which no plagues occur, tends to take it out of the public eye until trouble erupts. In the absence of sustained research and the maintenance of equipment and trained teams the cost of the plague, which is then bound to occur will dwarf the short term economies.

More insect pests strike at agriculture than at any other aspect of man's economy, and all we can do here is to point out a few of the problems that are involved. Every crop has pests either exclusive to it or, more often, shared to a greater or lesser degree with others, and may be attacked at all stages of its growth, so that no single treatment will suffice. It will be more useful to consider one important crop in some detail than to make many superficial comments in a fruitless attempt at generalization.

Pests of wheat

In Britain most wheat is sown in the autumn, for harvesting in August. Soil conditions may oblige the farmer to delay sowing from October until as late as February, but in a good year most of the seed will be in by early December. We shall see the importance of the timing in relation to insect pest attack.

Wheat may be attacked near the base at the seedling stage by wireworms, the larvae of click-beetles (Coleoptera: Elateridae) and if the crop is being grown on newly ploughed pasture land by leatherjackets, the larvae of crane-flies (Diptera: Tipulidae). The young plant may then suffer from the attack of the leaf beetle *Lema melanopa* (Coleoptera: Chrysomelidae) whose adults and larvae damage the leaves, and the wheat bulb fly, *Leptohylemyia coarctata* (Diptera: Muscidae) whose larva destroys the growing point. The fully-grown plants can be destroyed by the larvae of the wheat stem sawfly, *Cephus pygmaeus* (Hymenoptera: Tenthredinidae) or by the larva of the Hessian fly, *Mayetiola destructor* (Diptera: Cecidomyidae). The plants which survive may then have their heads destroyed by the caterpillars of the rustic shoulder knot moth, *Hadena basilinea* (Lepidoptera) which feeds on the grains. At any stage aphid attack may weaken the plants and reduce the size of the heads. The effects of the pests are illustrated diagrammatically in Figure 6.7. This list of possible disasters is by no means complete and after harvest the stored grain may be destroyed by beetles as described on page 176.

In practice the effects of the pests are minimized by combining good cultural practice, based on the crop's growth habits and the insects' ecological requirements, with the use of as little insecticide as possible. The second point is not only environmentally desirable but financially attractive to the farmer. The seed will probably have been dressed with a Lindane preparation before sowing. If the crop is to be grown on newly ploughed grassland the soil may first be sprayed with a BHC preparation as a protection against leatherjackets, and a similar precaution may be taken if the soil is known to harbour a large population of wireworms. The BHC can be applied in the form of pellets in which the insecticide is incorporated into a grain base that attracts the leatherjackets away from the crop. The technique is useful when the danger and crop stage are critical because it affords a quick and

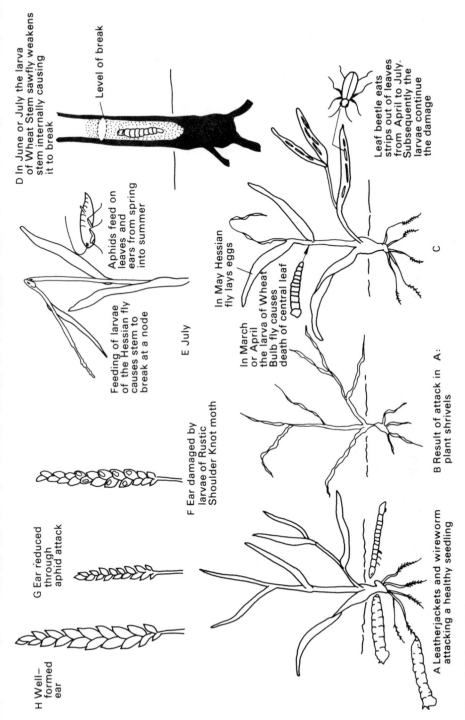

D In June or July the larva of Wheat Stem sawfly weakens stem internally causing it to break

Level of break

Aphids feed on leaves and ears from spring into summer

Feeding of larvae of the Hessian fly causes stem to break at a node

In May Hessian fly lays eggs

In March or April the larva of Wheat Bulb fly causes death of central leaf

Leaf beetle eats strips out of leaves from April to July. Subsequently the larvae continue the damage

C

E July

F Ear damaged by larvae of Rustic Shoulder Knot moth

B Result of attack in A: plant shrivels

G Ear reduced through aphid attack

H Well-formed ear

A Leatherjackets and wireworm attacking a healthy seedling

Figure 6.7 Pests of wheat

reliable control. The danger from wireworms can, however, be greatly reduced by not including grass in the rotation, for in nature they feed principally on the roots of grasses — a good reason for keeping couch-grass out of all arable land quite apart from other benefits which its removal confers. To reduce the size of a wireworm population by cultural methods takes time because wireworms remain in the soil as larvae for four or five years and feed on many crops besides cereals. The effect of attack by wireworms or leatherjackets is death of the young plants which cannot withstand the damage done to their roots by the latter while the former actually bite through the base of the tender stem and sever it from the root.

The wheat bulb fly lays its eggs on bare soil from midsummer onwards, and overwintering occurs in the egg stage. The larvae which emerge in late January and early February enter the young shoots and destroy the growing point, the first visible sign of attack being the yellowing and withering of the central leaf. Consequently a crop which can be brought on early is less likely to be attacked than a slightly later one, and it is worth taking the trouble of doing so because even dressed seed will not withstand a heavy attack and, should one occur, the farmer will either have to accept big losses or go to the expense of an early spring spraying which could have been avoided.

It pays too to drill not more than 2.5cm deep in order to expose the larvae to the action of the seed dressing. Much trouble can be averted by taking into account the females' oviposition habits and not growing winter wheat on ground which has been left bare, either as fallow or because the previous crops entailed a sizeable amount of bare ground at oviposition time — early potatoes for example. From this point of view the most suitable crop to precede wheat is one which gives good ground cover; other cereals, beans or grass. On the other hand, to precede wheat with grass invites leatherjackets! In nature the wheat bulb larva feeds on couch-grass, so that the conscientious farmer is to some extent at the mercy of his less careful neighbour.

The crop is relatively safe from further major insect pests until the summer, though it may suffer from leaf beetle attack. The beetle feeds in nature on several grasses including cocksfoot and couch. The adults emerge from hibernation in April and eggs are laid on the leaves until the end of July. Both adults and larvae bite longitudinal strips out of the leaves, the former causing the greater damage because the plants are young at the beginning of their attack. Early sowing helps, since the older the plants the more successfully will they withstand the loss of photosynthetic area.

In the summer the wheat stem sawfly may attack the crop. The adults emerge in June and lay one egg in each stem. The larva feeds on the pith and gradually moves towards the base of the stem which it plugs with debris and excrement. Then it cuts round the inner circumference of the stem which is so weakened that it snaps off just above the larval cell. At harvest the larva in its cell is undisturbed and remains until the following summer when it pupates. Stubble burning is an effective way of destroying the overwintering larvae, but since in nature the species attacks common grasses there is an abundant reservoir for subsequent attacks. At the same time as sawfly damage is seen the Hessian fly may produce stem breakage, but it is not a serious pest in Britain because autumn wheat is sown late and consequently avoids attack by the fly in autumn; whereas in warmer countries there are two broods in Britain there is only one. The adults emerge in May from pupae which overwintered. Eggs are laid on the stems or leaves and the larvae travel towards the leaf sheath at one of the lower nodes where they feed on the sap of the stem. After about a month they pupate on the node. As a result of the weakening of the stem by the larvae the whole plant is stunted, and the stem folds over at the affected node. After harvest the pupae remain among the stubble, and can be killed by burning.

A greater danger comes from aphids. Throughout the early spring and summer they suck from the leaves and stems and, at fruiting, even the ears. Attack is particularly dangerous when the ears are filling out and the grains are still at the milky stage. Under these conditions the loss can be up to two or three hundredweight per acre. Aphid attack on wheat has increased in recent years and can now be a source of serious loss. The insects do not transmit disease but by depriving the plants of nourishment appreciably reduce the size of the ears.

Finally loss may be caused by caterpillars of the rustic shoulder knot moth. They overwinter in the soil and in the spring move on to the plants. They attack the leaves and bore into the stems, killing them. The larvae may also attack the ears of surviving plants, eating out the grains. The moth attacks many grasses and is common, but not usually a serious pest.

From this account it may seem incredible that any wheat crop should ever yield a harvest. In practice not all the pests are active every year in all parts of the country, and the real danger lies in wireworms, leatherjackets, the wheat bulb fly and aphids. The farmer may be able to confine his insecticides to the original seed dressing and perhaps one spraying with Lindane or an organo-phosphate in the early summer, depending on what he observes as the season progresses. If he detects aphid attack alone he may decide to use a carbamate insecticide, pirimicarb, whose very low toxicity to other organisms makes it environmentally inoffensive. We have taken the example of wheat in some detail to show how a knowledge of pest ecology can be used to good purpose. The farmer cannot be expected to possess the detailed knowlege, if only because it is constantly changing; the behaviour of organisms is not governed by the textbooks, and even in relatively small-scale agriculture, as practised in Britain, sustained research is necessary — linked with an effective advisory service.

Forestry pests

Most Orders include some pests of forest trees. The damage which they do ranges from minor retardation of growth to complete destruction, the latter being generally due to micro-organisms transmitted by the insects. The list of pests is long, so we shall confine ourselves to a few which merit attention either because of the seriousness of the damage which they cause or because their activity reveals points of particular biological interest.

Chemical control has only limited value against forestry pests both on grounds of cost, since the size of the area to be covered entails the use of large quantities of insecticide, and for environmental reasons since the spraying usually has to be done from the air and is therefore indiscriminate, The Forestry Commission still uses a limited amount of DDT in nurseries but for almost all purposes BHC has replaced it. BHC is used extensively, mixed with the soil, against the larvae of Scarabeidae. Whereas in natural woodland these larvae (or *white grubs*, Figure 3.5: 6) feed on grass roots under the forest floor, in nurseries they feed on tree roots with fatal effects on the seedlings. BHC is a more acceptable control than DDT since it remains active in the soil for a shorter time, but it is an extremly powerful insecticide and the use of suitable forestry techniques is preferable. It is possible to avoid damage from *Melolontha* larvae by siting the nurseries on heathland, where conifers often grow well and the absence of broad-leaved trees makes the habitat unsuitable for adult cockchafers, which in turn reduces the number of larvae.[8] Climate, too, is an important consideration. In Britain the adult cockchafer is not a serious pest because the population is too small to act as a defoliator, but in continental Europe where the climate permits regular swarming it can be a serious defoliator. In these circumstances limited application of chlorinated hydrocarbons from the air may be justified.

The principal Orders which include forest pests are the Hymenoptera, Lepidoptera, Coleoptera, Hemiptera and Diptera; of these the beetles are by far the most important, followed by the Lepidoptera.

The British public has recently been made aware of forest pests by the outbreak of Dutch elm disease which is caused by a fungus, *Ceratocystis ulmi*, transmitted by two species of bark beetles. The disease had existed in Britain for about fifty years in a mild form which caused only a little fatal damage, but in the late 1960s a very aggressive strain appeared after the importation of infested elm logs from Canada: in less than eight years some three million trees were killed which was a serious loss since elms are an important scenic feature of rural Britain as well as being valuable timber trees.[9] Bark beetles spend their entire larval period in, or just under, the bark. The females excavate a short tunnel into the bark and then at right angles to it, a main tunnel which is enlarged in one place to form a mating chamber. After mating the female cuts niches in the side of the main tunnel and oviposits in them. The grubs then extend their cavities laterally to the main tunnel and at their ends make pupal chambers (Figure 6.8). The newly-emerged adults bore their way out of the bark in midsummer and then attack the elms forming a second generation which overwinters as larvae in the bark. The large elm bark beetle, *Scolytus scolytus*, attacks the trunk and larger branches, the smaller *S. multistriatus* makes its tunnels in the smaller branches. Their effects are similar. The fungus acts as a poison and also stimulates the xylem vessels to produce tyloses so that death from water shortage may occur. A light infestation usually causes no worse damage than dieback of branches in the first year, but a heavy one can kill healthy trees. Control of this disease was not successful in the south of England because sanitation felling could not keep up with the spread of the insects which are good fliers, and it is being allowed to work itself out. Completely healthy trees stand a fair chance of surviving, and since the disease is much less common in the north its further spread

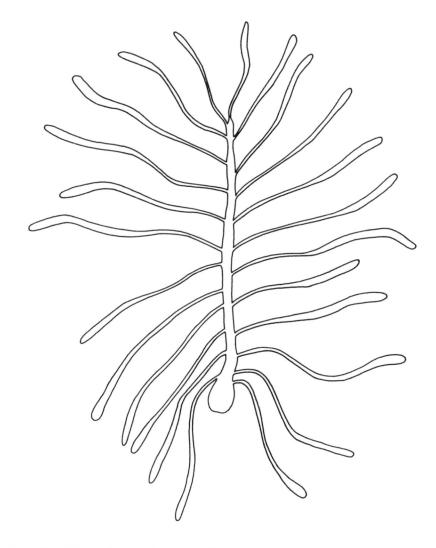

Figure 6.8 *Galleries of the elm bark beetle,* Scolytus scolytus

in Britain is controlled mainly by enforcing rigorous standards on the movement of elm logs within the country and on imported elm logs, both of which have to be treated with BHC. A long term solution is to breed resistant clones, but that is not yet a practical possibility.

Other genera of bark beetles attack oak and ash but are not of great economic importance. Conifers are very susceptible. Serious economic damage is done to the Scots pine, *Pinus sylvestris,* by the pine shoot beetle *Blastophagus* (or *Myelophilus*) *piniperda.* No associated fungus is involved with this pest; the beetle itself is the danger. Again, slightly damaged or sickly trees, or even fallen timber, are more likely to serve as breeding sites than is healthy timber, but in nature most trees are to some extent damaged and therefore susceptible. The pine shoot beetle makes galleries not unlike those of *Scolytus*. In early summer large numbers of adults emerge and immediately feed on the leading shoots, thereby stunting entire trees since pines, having monopodial growth, cannot produce well developed stems in the absence of the leading shoots. Good forestry practice can do much to alleviate the damage, for example by keeping the forest clear of potential breeding sites such as unbarked logs and sickly trees. After felling it is important to remove the felled material before the start of the next breeding season, and bark removed from logs should be burned.

The ambrosia beetles are atypical bark beetles inasmuch as they tunnel not in the bark, but extensively in the wood itself..Their tunnels are very small, so that the insects are know as pinhole borers. Not only do the tunnels reduce the commercial value of the wood but the emergence holes permit the entry of fungal spores from which even more serious damage may ensue. The beetles are pests on logs, some species affecting conifer wood, others hardwoods. They can be controlled by spraying the logs with BHC.

The pine weevil, *Hylobius abietis* (Figure 4.19), is a major pest of conifers generally and of *Pinus sylvestris* in particular. The adults live for two or more years, which is extremely rare among insects, and consequently large numbers are available as soon as activity begins in early spring because the overwintering adults are soon joined by the newly-emerging brood. The adults immediately attack either fallen wood, feeding on the bark and destroying the cambium, or else the upper branches of trees from five to twenty metres high which they damage in the same way. The result of their attack on the crowns resembles that of attack by the pine shoot beetle. The beetle finds great scope in plantations. In nature it does less damage for it exists in smaller numbers because it lays its eggs in severed wood which is partly or even wholly buried. In nature such habitats are less numerous than in cultivation when, especially after clear-felling, many stumps remain in the ground and can be used for oviposition for several years. Not even partial burning renders the stumps unsuitable. The larvae burrow deep into the wood where they overwinter. They pass through a brief pupal stage in early summer and the adults emerge by cutting large circular tunnels to the surface. The larvae do not therefore damage wood directly themselves: the adult is the injurious stage. A fairly effective control is to postpone replanting clear-felled areas for three or four years in order to give the stump population time to work itself out, but not only does that delay the re-use of valuable ground but it is thought that the soil may deteriorate in the meantime. The usual practice is to replant immediately with young trees which have been dipped in BHC, and subsequently to spray them. A new insecticide, chlorpyrifos, is beginning to replace BHC for this purpose.

The other group of beetles which provides forest pests is the Cerambycidae. The longhorn beetles lay their eggs in cracks in the bark and the larvae burrow for a while under the bark. They then bore elliptical holes into the wood sometimes penetrating deep into the heartwood where the larval stages may last for several years. Timber which has been extensively pierced in this way is of no commercial value. In Britain the longhorns are not serious pests although the larvae of some species kill young poplars and willows by tunnelling right round the stem, ringing it.

The most serious lepidopteran forest pest in Britain is probably the pine looper moth, *Bupalus piniarius,* which has for long been a serious pest of pine forests in northern, eastern and central Europe. Its caterpillars are defoliators of Scots pine and of many other conifers, and can devastate large forests. Pines are not able to withstand defoliation in two successive years and, since the moth may exist in large numbers, it is likely to present the trees with a challenge which they cannot resist. The first serious attack in Britain occurred in Cannock Chase in 1953, causing grave losses because although the moths' infestation lasted only one year it was followed by a secondary infestation of the weakened trees by the pine shoot beetle. The attack was probably confined to 1953 because in the following year the forest was sprayed with DDT from the air, but nowadays a less harmful insecticide, tetrachlorvinphos, is used for the purpose. A lower kill is achieved than by using DDT, but the population is reduced sufficiently to allow natural enemies to keep the pest in check. This kind of co-operation with nature is known as integrated control. A better long term solution to the pine looper moth problem lies in appropriate silvicultural planning. The risk to Scots pine is greatest where rainfall is very low, and on sandy soils underlain by hardpan. If such areas cannot be avoid‧. ed the danger can be reduced by appropriate soil treatment which in the short term, is costly.[10]

The Hymenoptera provide many forest pests but none in Britain is of great importance. The least serious are the social wasps whose adults sometimes do a little damage by stripping bark for making their nests. Sawfly caterpillars are sometimes defoliators of pine and larch, but the most serious harm is done by woodwasps whose larvae attack both conifers and deciduous trees. The woodwasp *Sirex gigas* damages wood mechanically because the larvae burrow deep. It is not really a serious pest of well maintained woodland since only weak trees are attacked; in healthy trees the flow of sap is too strong for successful oviposition.

The presence of woodwasps in large numbers is a sign of bad forest conditions which include dampness and fungal diseases, and woodwasps can serve as useful indicators. Two of the parasitic Hymenoptera, the ichneumon *Rhyssa persuasoria* and the cynipid *Ibalia leucospoides* which lay their eggs in the larvae act as natural controls. As in the case of many forest pests the solution to the problem lies in good management rather than with chemical control.

Termites are major pests of standing trees in some areas and damage timber structures in most tropical regions. Mature indigenous trees are rarely threatened, but termites do much damage to trees in nurseries and to young ones in the field because even those whose wood is inimical to termite attack need to attain a certain age before their resistance is achieved.

In Africa *Eucalyptus,* a very important timber tree, is particularly susceptible to attack. The damage is done mainly by species which make their nests on or in the ground and damage the roots. In India teak, *Tectonia grandis,* in Eastern Australia *Eucalyptus* and in South America mahogany, *Swietenia macrophylla,* are vulnerable. In the case of mahogany the timber of adult trees is damaged by channels being excavated through the living wood. In addition to these particularly important ones most trees are attacked, for the list of resistant species is comparatively short. Trees are more vulnerable in the dry than in the wet season especially when they are young, because they are then less able to recover from root damage which may also severely restrict the regeneration of woodland in semi-arid regions. *Eucalyptus* is often grown for making poles and after felling, the stumps regenerate by coppicing. Termites, however, may cover the stumps with earth, or else destroy the root systems which grow from the new shoots for which reason the stumps have to be treated with a wood preservative which deters them, and the cost of such laborious treatment in a large plantation may be considerable. Chlorinated hydrocarbons mixed with the soil have been found to have a repellent action on termites and, owing to their residual properties, can be used in small quantities. By using BHC or dieldrin it has been possible to establish *Eucalyptus*, which is important not only as a timber tree but, because it grows fast, as a wind-break and in the rehabilitation of over-cultivated land.

Pests of stored products

Pests which damage stored products at various stages between the producer and the consumer are the cause of great economic loss. Such losses are almost impossible to quantify but it is estimated that at the present time between five and ten per cent of the world cereal crop is destroyed by insect pests *after* harvesting — apart from losses due to rodents.

The principal pests are shown in Figure 6.9. They are the adults and larvae of beetles and the caterpillars of moths: a few Hymenoptera and Diptera cause damage, but very little by comparison. By far the most serious are the weevils which cause vast losses annually on a world-wide scale. They are *Sitophilus granarius, S. oryzae* and *S. zeamais* which infest wheat, rice and maize respectively. The larvae hatch from eggs that are laid by adults on the field crop. They complete their larval development in the stored grain, and when adults appear they produce further generations. It is often necessary to store grain in bulk for a long time which increases the risk of damage and also reduces the efficacy of fumigation as a means of control owing to the possibility of re-infestation from new deliveries of grain to the warehouse. There is a simple solution, expensive initially because it calls for specially constructed containers but profitable in the long run because of low maintenance costs, namely air-tight storage. Containers made out of concrete, underground, and properly roofed are suitable for the storage of dry grain. A certain amount of loss has to be accepted, but after some time the carbon dioxide emitted by the live wheat, and to a lesser extent by the insects, acts as a poison on weevils which die even before all the oxygen has been consumed and before they have had time to do very much damage. The method is doubly valuable since it has advantages beyond insect pest control: it disposes of rodents too and prevents re-infestation and over-heating. Grain which is not stored under air-tight conditions has to be shifted in order to avoid over-heating, which calls for labour or special machinery.

Air-tight storage can be used with advantage even with wet grain. Although it is unlikely to be fit for human consumption, loss due to pests is eliminated and

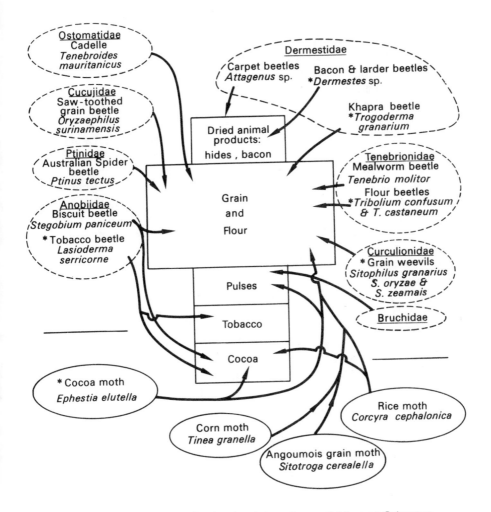

Figure 6.9 *Pests of stored products* Species placed above the parallel lines are Coleoptera, those below them are Lepidoptera. Major pests only are shown: asterisks indicate those whose economic importance is greatest

the grain is used as cattle feed. Barley and oats are treated in this manner in welded steel silos.

That type of control is a good example of the way in which initial outlay can serve many purposes.

Grain weevils are pests of unmilled grain and so are the saw-toothed grain beetle and the Khapra beetle. The saw-toothed grain beetle illustrates how agricultural practice can be adapted to overcome a pest. It occurs especially on farms where grain is dried rather quickly at harvest time by warming it. If it is then immediately stored it is in just the right condition for beetles which have entered to breed. The problem can be overcome by blowing cool air into the grain as soon as the drying process has been completed.

Many stored products insects are cosmopolitan, being spread in the course of trade. Even tropical species can exist in temperate climates under warehouse conditions, although some are unable to breed there. The Khapra beetle is a good example of a widely distributed pest, originating in India and now occurring in Europe, the USA and parts of Africa. It infests wheat, maize, rice, ground-nuts and other products, being difficult to detect on account of its small size, from two to three millimetres, and cryptic colouration in both adult and larval stages. Its success is enhanced by its adaptability not only to a varied diet but also to a wide range of temperature and humidity, and to sudden changes in them. An important factor in the ability of the larvae to survive is their use of diapause, a state of suspended animation. Diapause is a common phenomenon, but usually it forms a set part of an insect's development and is not of great duration. In the Khapra larva, however, it is induced by extremes of temperature, desiccation or starvation and can last for as long as eight years. A ship which has carried an infested cargo may continue to carry the pest concealed in inaccessible places. Subsequent clean cargoes may therefore become infested, while the insects are carried across the world. Fumigation of a ship's hold has to be very thorough if all the well concealed insects are to be killed, and even if a long time should pass before it next carries a cargo of stored products diapause will enable the larvae to survive.

Several moths infest grain: Figure 6.9. shows only a few of the most serious ones. Again, a knowledge of their behaviour is the key to controlling them. The widespread *Ephestia elutella* is held in check successfully enough by means of spraying residual insecticides (BHC or malathion) in warehouses, because the larvae do not spend their entire life inside the grain. They travel around the warehouse, where they are liable to be poisoned. Their high reproductive rate however, calls for constant vigilance; imperfect spraying can lead to a rapid rise in numbers. *Sitotroga cerealella* on the other hand, spends its entire larval life within the grain so that infestation can neither be detected at an early stage nor readily controlled by spraying. However, since it usually infests the crop at harvest time its danger can be minimized by early harvesting and threshing.

Some species feed on milled flour rather than on grain. The most serious are the flour beetles, *Tribolium confusum* and *T. castaneum.* They are tropical and, although virtually cosmopolitan cannot survive winter in temperate climates except in heated premises. Re-infestation, however, occurs continually through fresh imports, for the beetles' small size (about five millimetres) often allows them to escape detection. Other pests of milled flour are the cadelle, *Tenebroides mauritanicus,* which in addition to eating a certain amount of flour causes even more loss by feeding on the fabric of the sacks, the biscuit beetle *Stegobium paniceum,* and the Australian spider beetle, *Ptinus tectus.* The distinction into species which feed on whole grain and those which eat milled flour is far from rigid; most species will consume either and attack other products as well.

In addition to the control measures already described a highly effective method exists for pests of milled flour. The Entoleter is a machine which makes use of centrifugal force for the mechanical destruction of pests. Flour shot into the machine is flung between metal discs revolving at 2900 rpm, and against metal studs, with such force that all stages of insects, including their eggs, are destroyed. The method gives almost complete control of the most important beetle and lepidopteran pests, and by using the machine at even greater speed is effective for grain as well as for flour.

Pests of manufactured articles

The most important manufactured articles to be attacked by insects are timber structures, principally railway sleepers, telegraph poles, the fabric of buildings and furniture. The principal pests are termites, furniture beetles (woodworm) and some moths.

On page 175 we considered termites as forestry pests. They do far more damage to timber structures than to trees. The reason that some timber trees are particularly vulnerable to attack is that they lack natural resistance. A certain amount of mystery surrounds resistance, for a species which resists termite attack in nature may be susceptible when it is used as timber. The substances which repel termites are not evenly distributed in a tree so that the resistance of timber can depend on the part of the tree from which it was cut. High lignin content is a deterrent since termites cannot digest lignin, which means that in general the heartwood of hardwood trees provides the safest naturally protected timbers. On account of the large number of termite species it is possible that a timber which has proved to be resistant in one place may not be so elsewhere. The manner of treating timber to make it resistant is a question of timber technology rather than entomology, so we need not dwell on it beyond pointing out that it is costly because to be effective it requires the use of dipping tanks or pressure impregnation equipment, and involves additional transport and handling costs.

The way in which termites attack not only timber buildings, but wooden structures in buildings which are constructed principally of other materials, is related to their biology. Termites are more particular than most insects about temperature and especially about humidity, a feature which is related to the equable conditions which they maintain in their nests. The dry-wood termites treat structural timber as normal nesting material, excavating galleries along the grain. The colony is founded by a pair of winged termites penetrating at some unprotected point and then producing the first brood of nymphs which enlarge the nest. No external signs are visible at first because termites are negatively phototactic for most of the time and all their requirements can be found within the wood. Eventually the first visible sign of infestation appears, small holes made to the exterior, through which the accumulated faecal pellets are expelled. Because the dry-wood termites live in small colonies the damage which they do is slow in making itself felt, but if further colonies are founded the cumulative effect can be disastrous especially if the timbers which are being attacked form the sub-structure of a building. In some circumstances the warning signs of faecal pellets may not be observed and the first intimation of trouble is the collapse of the floor, or worse. The dry-wood genus *Cryptotermes* is a major pest in most tropical and sub-tropical areas, individual species being widespread owing to transport by man. For protection against these termites, which attack after landing from the air, it is particularly necessary to use treated timber in house building. Even so infestation can be brought in with furniture or packing cases for some termites nest under the outer laminations of plywood. An infested building can be fumigated with methyl bromide after covering it entirely in plastic sheeting, but it is a costly and dangerous process.

It is easier, theoretically, to protect a building against the many species of termite which invade from the ground. Most of them are subterranean, some are mound-builders. None of them actually nests in timber, but they infest timber structures in order to obtain wood which is then carried back to the nest. Their colonies are much larger than those of the dry-wood species, so that their effect is much more rapidly felt. The nest may be a hundred metres from their source of timber and, owing to the termites' dislike of moving in the open, any part of their journey which has to be made over some impenetrable material, such as a concrete foundation, is made into a covered way. A little tunnel of masticated wood or other material is extended from the nest to the building. The covered ways, if detected, enable the owners of the building to take precautions. Many houses in tropical countries are built on piles, often of wood in which case the termites will work their way up internally. If the piles are of dark brick the covered ways may not be conspicuous. Mound-builders may build their mound under an elevated building and, when the mound reaches the floor, enter it undetected from below. The mound-builders are extremely dangerous because they completely excavate the inside of timber leaving only the thinnest envelope. Having hollowed the wood they may give the weakened structure temporary reinforcement by filling it in with soil mixed with saliva, but sudden collapse ensues. Because of the large numbers of individuals at work all this can happen quite quickly.

If money presented no problem simple technology could overcome the danger of infestation from the ground. The site should first be treated with chlorinated hydrocarbons, and ideally a concrete foundation should be laid of such an area that some concrete remains unenclosed outside the walls of the building. At about half a metre from the ground a termite shield should extend right round the building. The shield consists of a strip of metal projecting five centimetres from the side of the building, and bent downwards, presenting termites with an insuperable barrier. If a house is built on pillars each pillar should be similarly equipped. If, in addition only treated timber is used, and care is taken to avoid all direct unprotected connexions with the ground such as steps, plumbing or cables the house is reasonably secure. All these precautions, however, are costly and are often not implemented in areas of low-cost housing.

Apart from timber buildings termites destroy many manufactured articles. All the species which eat the timber of buildings will similarly eat other materials made of cellulose; books, documents and fibre cloth of all kinds. These losses are serious both economically and culturally. Termites have been known to bite through soft metal, especially lead which is used for sheathing electric cables. Many plastics, used for the same purpose and for packaging are vulnerable.

It is notoriously difficult to express the cost of pests to man's economy in any useful manner. It is impossible to assess the effect of termite damage to pasture in real terms but an attempt can be made to quantify the damage done to timber structures in developed countries where records are available. At a symposium of the British Wood Preserving Association in 1966, Dr Norman Hickin gave the approximate annual cost of termites in the USA as £208 000 000, and in Australia as £2 300 000 for the State of Queensland alone.

Termites are amongst the greatest of pests. Their effects are less dramatic than those of the vectors of disease, and no one dies of starvation because of their agricultural importance: they are not like a plague of locusts. They are small and keep largely out of sight but, through the damage which they do to grassland, they are a factor in lowering the quality of life for many pastoral peoples and, in their effect on manufactured articles, insidious and only occasionally spectacular, they apply a brake on the development of a country's potential.

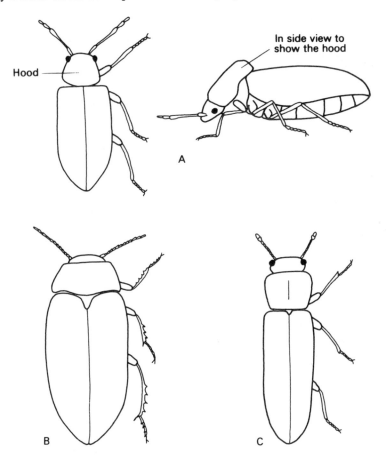

Figure 6.10 *Wood-boring beetles* A common furniture beetle (Anobiidae) B death-watch beetle (Anobiidae) C powder-post beetle (Lyctidae)

Compared with the work of termites the effect of wood-boring beetles is slight, but it does cause considerable economic loss. Unlike the termites the beetles do not destroy timber structures wholesale, they weaken them and spoil furniture. They are members of the Families Anobiidae, furniture beetles, and Lyctidae, powder-post beetles (Figure 6.10). The eggs are laid just under the surface of the wood and damage is done by the larvae which burrow into and actually feed on it. In their gut anobiid larvae harbour symbiotic yeasts which are associated with the break-down of cellulose and they can digest dry heartwood. They are, therefore, pests of seasoned timber whilst lyctid larvae, being devoid of cellulases, must rely on the starch content of the wood and are confined to the sapwood of fresh timber. The larval period of the Anobiidae is long: in *Anobium punctatum*, the common furniture beetle, it may last up to three years and in *Xestobium rufo-villosum*, the death-watch beetle, up to ten years at about 20^0 C. During this time the larval burrows penetrate deep. When they are ready to pupate the larvae work their way outwards, forming pupal cells just below the surface. The adults bite their way out and emerge through small holes. The appearance on the surface of structural timber or furniture of the small emergence holes is usually the first sign of infestation although if a large number of *Anobium* emerge together some will probably be found in the building. In the case of *Xestobium*, the characteristic knocking sound which both sexes make as a mating signal by striking their heads against the wood may serve as a warning. *Anobium* is much the commoner of the two. Its economic effect is mainly on the appearance of timber and furniture since the larval tunnels do not penetrate deep enough to weaken any but slender structures. Almost any type of wood can be attacked. *Xestobium* is much more destructive, especially in oak. It selects damp wood, and the larvae burrow deep. For these reasons it is a menace to historic buildings, especially tall ones whose roofs are not regularly inspected and where the timbers have been weakened by water and fungal attack. The tunnelling can be so extensive as to cause collapse. It seems certain that all existing death-watch infestation has arisen from larvae that were present in the timbers when they were incorporated into buildings, and no new infestations arise.

Lyctus attacks timber shortly after felling when the water content has fallen slightly, and before it has become too low since the beetle has very restricted humidity requirements. The timber is attacked either in the forest, or in the yard after it has been sawn into planks, and the infestation may not be detected until after it has been used in building or as furniture. The eggs are laid in the xylem vessels, wood such as birch and beech whose vessels are too narrow for oviposition being immune to attack.

The wood-boring beetles are excellent examples of free-living insects, which perform a useful ecological function, becoming pests. In nature they play a part in the early stages of decomposition of dead wood in the forest, and become pests when wood is used as timber. Infestation may arise from adults living in nature. In England houses in areas which contain much old standing oak are often attacked in that way, but it is readily caused by infested furniture being brought into 'clean' houses.

The control of wood-boring beetles is governed by their various requirements. In the case of *Xestobium* the treatment must include damp-proofing precautions to discourage fungal action, together with the application of a suitable woodworm fluid (BHC together with a solvent in an oil as carrier) both brushed on and injected. If the timbers are very large injection holes are drilled to over half their thickness. Similar insecticidal treatment is needed against *Anobium* in structural timbers, although it need not involve injection to so great a depth. In furniture *Anobium* often bores into the plywood parts of drawers and cupboards, which are best removed and replaced with hardboard, the fluid being brushed on to the remainder of the article and injected into the beetles' emergence holes. Similar brushing and injection is appropriate against *Lyctus,* with the additional precaution of removing as far as possible all the infested sap-wood and burning it.

Several moths have adapted themselves to feeding, in the larval stage, on the hair, feathers and skin of dead animals. They acted as useful scavengers in nature because they disposed of highly keratinized structures which few other animals were able to digest. Unfortunately the animal fibres which man uses for clothing and furnishings are equally suitable for the larvae which can be serious pests of woollen clothing, carpets, furs and feathers both in warehouses and in use. Materials which are used in the home or in shops and hotels are particularly vulnerable because they are likely to become soiled with food or sweat, under which conditions the moths are better able to breed than if the materials are completely clean.

The most highly adapted of all the house moths is the clothes moth, *Tineola bisselliella,* which displays extreme adaptation to its atypical lepidopteran way of life: it is also by far the most serious pest. The adaptation is so profound that in the adult there is no trace of the sucking proboscis which is universally present in all but the most primitive Lepidoptera (Figure 4.31 page 90). The drably-coloured wings have a ragged appearance, perhaps an example of crypsis, and the insect has poor powers of flight. Most of the clothes moths that are seen fluttering about are males: the females scarcely fly so that the householder's energetic pursuit of the flying moth is largely wasted effort. Both sexes, however, have strong legs equipped with many spines and can run fast: in addition the males can jump using their hind-legs and a little help from the wings. These adaptations are valuable for what is essentially a ground-living insect. The females lay between forty and fifty eggs which adhere lightly to the surface. The larvae are not typical lepidopteran caterpillars. They lack ocelli but exhibit negative phototaxis. With their powerful mandibles they sever the fibres, usually eating only a little but causing great damage to the material. They may spin themselves delicate tubes of silk inside which they move, or may crawl about unprotected. When they are ready to ecdyse, and when about to pupate, they make more elaborate tents outside the silken tube. The tents incorporate the debris of fibres and give good camouflage. The life cycle takes about a hundred days at 25^0C.

In the home the best control measures are a combination of cleanliness and some insecticidal treatment. Any carpet or upholstery of animal fibre which is left undisturbed, under heavy furniture for example, is likely to be infested and so are woollen clothes that are stored in a soiled condition. Furs should be shaken out periodically and examined. Moth balls of naphthalene or para-dichlor-benzene are effective as fumigants provided that they are enclosed with clothes in air-tight plastic containers: it is useless just to put a few in a wardrobe. In warehouses infestations can be overcome by fumigation, but to guard against re-infestation from materials subsequently brought in calls for frequent inspection.

Conclusion

We have seen something of the insects' impact on man's economy. Insect pests impose a strain on our resources that is, literally, incalculable and whose end cannot be foreseen. We have still not learnt how to live with the rest of the natural world, and tend to go for the quick easy solution of indiscriminate killing rather than of collaboration. Biological control is bound to increase in importance now that the major insect hazards to health and agriculture have to a certain extent, been brought under control by chemical means. The future must lie with integrated control, not only on environmental grounds but for economy too since any new insecticide with acceptable environmental features is likely to be expensive. Intelligence and fore-sight are more valuable than ferocity as long-term weapons against pests. We have seen how insects not only possess adaptations to terrestrial life but, partly on acc-ount of their small size and high reproductive rate, have evolved and pushed adap-tive radiation to a degree exceeded by no other group of animals. The pest species are best of all at adaptation, which is largely why they have become pests and are difficult to overcome. It follows that as man defeats them in one way they will find alternative solutions and continue to present a challenge which can be met only by a combination of research of the most fundamental kind into their physiology, and its morphological basis, allied to research in ecology and the practical applications of methods of control.

References

1 ELLIOTT, M., JANES, N.F., NEEDHAM, P.H., PULMAN, D.A. and
   STEVENSON, J.H. (1973). NRDC 143, a more stable pyrethroid. Proceedings
   7th British Insecticide & Fungicide Conference.
2 Insecticides & Fungicides Department at Rothamsted. *Chemistry & Industry*
   21 December 1974.
3 DEBACH, P. (1974). *Biological control by natural enemies.* Cambridge
   University Press.
4 WATERHOUSE, D.F. The biological control of dung. *Scientific American*
   April 1974.
5 NASH, T.A.M. (1969). *Africa's bane: The tsetse fly.* London: Collins.
   This is a most readable book written in a semi-popular style by a leading
   authority.
   MULLIGAN, H.W. (Ed.) (1970). *The African trypanosomiases.* London: Allen
   & Unwin.

This book is a collection of authoritative articles which cover almost every aspect of the subject in detail.

MATTINGLY, P.F. (1969). *The biology of mosquito-borne disease*. London: George Allen & Unwin.

This is written by a leading authority.

(1958) *Mosquitoes and their relation to disease*. Economic series No. 4. 6th edition. London: British Museum (Natural History).

A useful short account.

GORDON SMITH, C.E. (Ed.) (1972). Research in diseases of the tropics. *Br. med. Bull.* 1.

This book contains much valuable but rather technical information.

6   CORNWELL, P.B. (July/August 1974). The incidence of fleas and bedbugs in Britain. *International pest control*.

Valuable sources of information on insects and hygiene generally are:

BUSVINE, J.R.(2nd edition 1966). *Insects and hygiene*. London: Methuen.

This covers a very wide range of disease-carrying and annoying insects, including clothes moths.

BUXTON, P.A. (1935, 2nd edition 1947). *The louse*. London: Edward Arnold.

This is an exciting book to read in spite of its date, having been written by a distinguished worker.

CORNWELL, P.B. (1968). *The cockroach*. London: Hutchinson.

LAPAGE, G. (1957). *Animals parasitic in man*. Penguin Books.

This readable book covers many groups besides insects, but includes plenty of information about vectors of disease.

7   HASKELL, P.T. (1970) The future of locust and grasshopper control. *Outlook on Agriculture*. vol.6 No.4. 166–174.

UVAROV, B.P. (1966). *Grasshoppers & locusts*. London: Cambridge University Press.

A most authoritative work. Only vol.1 has been published at the time of writing, but vol.2, which will deal with methods of control, is expected to appear in 1975. It will be the standard work in the English language.

HARRIS, W.V. (1961). *Termites: their recognition and control*. London: Longmans.

This describes all aspects of the economic importance of termites.

SMITH, K.M. (2nd edition 1948). *A textbook of agricultural entomology*. Cambridge University Press.

This book, although old, contains useful details of plant pests and the damage which they do in British agriculture.

HICKIN, N.E. (1971). *Termites: a world problem*. London: Hutchinson.

While it discusses the biology of termites generally this book places special emphasis on their role as destroyers of buildings.

8   PHILLIPS, D.H. (1974). *Control of diseases and invertebrate pests in forestry in Great Britain: chemicals and their alternatives*. London: Forestry Commission.

9   GIBBS, J.N. (1974). Forestry Commission, Forest Record No. 94. *Biology of Dutch elm disease*. London: H.M.S.O.

10 Forestry Commission—Leaflet No.32 (1959) *Pine looper moth.* London H.M.S.O.
    CHRYSTAL, R.N. (1937). *Insects of the British Woodlands*. London: Warne.
        Although out of date on methods of control this book contains valuable
        information about the biology of forest insects.
    MUNRO, J.W. (1966). *Pests of stored products*. London: Hutchinson.
        This is an authoritative work on the pest species and their control.

Index